What readers have written to Al Sicherman:

Over the years I feel as if you are one of the family. Yes, we are a strange family.

— *Lenore Campbell, Minnetonka*

In my universe, you are an American treasure.

— *Linda Falch, Richfield*

I hope you will be writing for as long as I'm able to read. (No pressure; I'm almost 73.)

— *Betty Wallien, Bloomington*

By using the teachings of our Uncle Al, we can laugh at ourselves— and know which Campbell's soup is best in our hot dish.

— *Jim Grell, Minneapolis*

In my mind, you are like a Minnesota version of James Thurber without all the annoying stylistic baggage.

— *Pete Havanac, Blaine*

I've really enjoyed reading your columns over the many years. They've been great. The talking dogs, the many trips to the hardware store, the food tidbits (the sometimes irrelevant parenthetical asides) have just been fun to read.

— *Dick Hendrickson, Minneapolis*

The Internet is full of data. A subset of this is plausible. A subset of that is informative. A subset of the information is knowledge. And a subset of the knowledge is wisdom. In the vast gulf between data and wisdom are many of your columns.

— *Jim Pemberton, Minneapolis*

Uncle Al's Geezer Salad

A mixed bag of reports on overlong repair projects, smart remarks from dogs and a whole lot of one man's decline into mental cottage cheese

AL SICHERMAN

Syren Book Company
Minneapolis, Minnesota

Published by
Syren Book Company
5120 Cedar Lake Road
Minneapolis, MN 55416
763-398-0030
www.syrenbooks.com

Printed in the United States of America on acid-free paper

ISBN 978-0-929636-80-1

LCCN 2007929925

Cover design by Kyle G. Hunter
Interior text design by Wendy Holdman
Cover photo by Catherine Watson

To order additional copies of this book, please go to www.itascabooks.com.

For Dave, Joe and Catherine, who have liked my stories.

For Kathy, John, Helen, Will, Elizabeth, James, Charlie, Jonathan, Rebecca, Emily, Andrew, Matt, Kurt and Karl—I really am their Uncle Al.

And for Lucky, Fuzzy and Gus, who would happily trade so great an honor as this dedication for half a cup of dry kibble.

Contents

ᴄᴄᴄ

Author's Note

For more than 18 years I wrote a weekly humor column for the *Minneapolis Star Tribune*. The column never had a name, nor anything to indicate that it was supposed to be funny (except my face, which is pretty laughable). I figured that if I didn't claim it was funny, people who weren't amused couldn't complain. (I was wrong.)

Striving always to be one step ahead of the millions of complaining letters and phone calls generated by my columns on any one subject, I attempted over time to shed light on a wide range of topics. But now, casting a jaundiced eye back over the more than 800 columns (Note to self: Get somebody to look at jaundiced eye), it is apparent that there have been themes in my life, to which the column frequently—if not productively—returned.

One of those themes—increasing geezerification—encompasses most of the others, from letting simple household repairs get out of hand, to speaking on behalf of dogs, to offering unsolicited analysis of the national and world economies. In fact, the longer I examine my life, the older—and the more geezerly—I get. My automotive habits don't yet include getting a better shot at a nice right turn by first moving to the left, but I can see the appeal. And since I retired, dinner has begun to sound good to me along about 4:30.

In any case, it is my hope that, by collecting a bunch of these peculiar tales and making them available in more permanent form for a planetwide audience, I can help others avoid the terrible mistakes that I have made. At the very least, others can make those mistakes anyway, but in full awareness of how many trips to the hardware store will be involved in the simplest project. And they can benefit from my finest gift: the solution to the mystery of underwear in the gutter.

Al Sicherman
Summer 2007

Acknowledgments

Thanks to friends Dick Parker and Sue Peterson, who listened to longer, stupider versions of all of these tales at numberless lunches; to friends Deb and Phil Ford for frequent (and amusing) advice; and to Sharon Emery and Martha Buns, Kathe Connair, Bill Hammond, Sharon Hodge, Maury Hobbs, Nicole Hvidsten, Tom Jones, Patty Pryor, Marci Schmitt, Jarrett Smith, Beth Thibodeau and others over time who made up "the crack Uncle Al Editing Team." If you think these stories are peculiar now, you should have seen them before they were edited.

Uncle Al's
Geezer Salad

Speak, Lucky! Or on Second Thought . . .

There are signs in our lives, if we but choose to see them, that all is not well with us.

Premature aging, for example, might be evidenced by an early desire to wear a hat while driving, or perhaps an urge to wear knee-high hosiery and a housedress to the office.

Signs of gastrointestinal problems to which you might want to pay attention include that others find the array of noises coming from your stomach unusual, or that you know more than any of your acquaintances do about the locations of various buildings' restrooms.

And if it seems to you that there has been a welcome reduction in the level of unwanted music coming at you from other people's cars, consider having your hearing tested.

Mental or emotional distress may be the hardest to recognize in ourselves because it dulls the very faculties that are required to recognize it. But a careful examination of changes in life patterns might disclose warning signs.

I bring this to our mutual breakfast table because I am a bit concerned about two things that happened to me recently. Both involve talking to Lucky, the household dog.

Now, as most pet owners will probably attest, there's nothing wrong—or even at all unusual—about talking to one's pet. "How're you doin', Spot?" or "Does my little Fluffikins want to go for her walkums?" are fairly common things to hear pet owners say.

And it isn't very unusual for the pet owners to imagine—or even to vocalize—the pet's response. Thus human beings can sometimes be heard saying, in the dog or cat's presumed voice, "I'm hungry!" or "I missed my Mommykins!"

So I have not been at all concerned that I often speak on Lucky's behalf.

I was, however, taken aback when the following occurred a few weeks ago:

I spilled some popcorn kernels on the kitchen floor, and Lucky rushed in, of course, to scarf up whatever had landed in his domain. I shooed him out of the kitchen while I swept up, because I was sure that unpopped popcorn wouldn't be good for him. When I glanced up, I saw him in the doorway, looking hurt because I had hollered.

So I said, "I'm sorry I hollered at you, Lucky, but we don't eat unpopped popcorn, because it could make us sick."

He responded, "Don't patronize me, Al."

And I replied, "I didn't mean to be patronizing, Lucky, it's just that . . ."

It was at that point I realized that something had gone terribly wrong in my conversational life.

But time, that great heeler (as dogs and shoemakers say), passed, and soon I had forgotten my concern.

Then a few days ago, I was relaxing with a book and the dog on my lap, when suddenly he switched into property-protection mode and began to leap around and bark endlessly at a squirrel out on the lawn.

"I liked it better when you were more contemplative, Luck," I observed.

His response, "Yeah, well, blow it out your patoot, Al," was so startling—and so unlike him—that I burst out laughing.

I feel bad on two counts:

One, I'm losing my mind.

Two, by laughing at the dog's outburst, I'm encouraging him to use bad language.

A Doubly Bang-Up Day

A little more than a year has passed, now, since the day I hit my own car twice. With my other car. Actually, I hit each one once with the other one. It wasn't one of my better days.

I tried to forget the Day of the Colliding Cars, but I was forced to remember it months later, in a way that let me know that my younger son, who hadn't been there when it happened, might one day be a detective.

I should begin by explaining that I have this second car that I keep in the one-car garage over the winter. That sounds pretty hoity-toity—and it certainly is a luxury—but the car isn't that great. It's not a classic in perfect condition. It's a 1971 Cutlass convertible, and it's rusting happily away.

I keep it in the garage over the winter only to keep it from rusting even faster, and because it's a pretty lousy winter car. You wouldn't believe how badly it does on a slippery hill. It also leaks water around the windshield, which is much more annoying in winter than in summer. It gets terrible gas mileage, so I don't drive it a lot even in the summer. It also needs a new torque converter. And three years ago I put more into having the engine rebuilt than the whole car was worth. And now it's worth even less than that.

So if you've stopped envying me this second car, let me also tell you that my regular car isn't worth a whole lot either. It's a seven-year-old compact pickup truck. But it looks pretty nice—or it did until one day a little more than a year ago.

It was a warmish Sunday in early spring, a good time to get the convertible out of the garage in any case, but there was an extra reason to do it that day. That afternoon we were to pick up Nan (my wife's grandmother) and Nan's daughter (my wife's aunt Lola), who was visiting from California, and take them to a gathering. The convertible was the vehicle of choice.

So early that morning I went into the garage and, squeezing past all the miscellaneous junk that also spends winters (and summers) there, got into the car, got it started after a few tries and—watching very carefully to make sure that neither front fender scraped against any of the protruding handles, shelves, wheels or knobs of the stuff that was stacked alongside—slowly backed it out.

Into the truck.

Not straight into it, though. The truck was parked next to the garage door. The rear bumper of the car scraped the right rear fender of the truck, and the rear bumper of the truck scraped the left rear fender of the car. If the two bumpers had been at the same height, each bumper might just have hit the other. But they weren't.

The scrape on the truck wasn't too bad. The car, being held together mostly by paint, did worse: A piece of chrome came off and a sizable hole, rimmed with rust flakes, appeared at one of the places where it had been fastened.

Ah, well, I thought (after several other, slightly briefer, thoughts), these things happen to cars, and at least there's nobody to blame but myself. So, grumbling a little, I moved the car around the truck and cleaned out the remnants of the previous summer and fall (leaves, hamburger wrappers, cheese-curl bags, etc.) from the floor of the back seat.

There! For better or worse, the car was ready to carry us, Nan and Lola to the party. Which it did, splendidly.

On the way back that evening, we decided to stop at our house, which Lola had never seen. I pulled up to a few feet behind the truck, and, realizing that the truck was blocking the steps, I got out and backed it up a couple of feet (making sure I didn't smack into the car) before we helped the ladies into the house.

I haven't mentioned before that our driveway slopes down slightly from the house to the street. I also didn't mention that somehow, in the excitement of moving the truck (I really need to get out more), I must have left it in neutral. Apparently, while we were in the house chatting, it quietly rolled back the foot or two that had separated it from the front of the car. No big deal.

At about 10 o'clock Nan and Lola decided that it was time to go, so we all got back into the car and I backed down the driveway the way any conscientious driver would—looking out the side and back windows for possible approaching traffic. It was only when I had finished backing into the street, stopped and turned my head that I saw the truck rolling down the driveway right after us.

Luckily the truck wasn't going very fast when it hit us, and nobody was at all hurt, although Nan, in the front passenger's seat, had seen it coming and was rather unnerved. I drove the truck back up the driveway, looked at the damage, which consisted of a pretty solid ding on the left front fender of the car and nothing much on the truck, and then I drove us to Nan's apartment.

On the way it seemed that there was something odd about the headlights, but nothing I could pinpoint. But when I

stopped the car at Nan's and shut off the engine, the headlights went out. A look under the hood confirmed that in the
collision a battery cable had pulled out of its clamp, and the
car's alternator had been running the lights until I stopped
the engine.

I reconnected the battery cable while my wife saw Nan and
Lola into the building (I carry tools—it's a 19-year-old car), and
that (aside from the various scrapes, dings and concerns about
my ability to drive) was that. I never embarrassed myself by
attempting to file an insurance claim, since neither car was
really worth it.

Months later (accident-free months, I should note), my son
Dave, who was then not quite 15 and living with his mother in
Milwaukee, was on a mini-vacation trip with me in the convertible. He gestured at the digital clock on the dashboard radio,
which never displays the right time because it's impossible to
reset without finding the radio's long-lost instructions (there
are no clock-related buttons—you do something like push
"Local/Distant" and "AM/FM" at the same time while putting
your right foot on your left ear). I had done it once, when I
bought the radio, but I had given up trying to remember how
to do it the first time it had to be changed to or from daylight
saving time.

"Hey, Dad," Dave asked, "what happened to your car at
10:15?"

I had no idea what he was talking about. "Nothing. What
do you mean?"

"Your clock is an hour and forty-five minutes fast. When
they get connected, they usually start at 12 o'clock, so this one
must have been reconnected some day or night at 10:15. Why
did you have your battery out?"

That's when I remembered the day I hit my own car twice and reconnected the battery at Nan's—at something like 10:15!

It was positively chilling. What else did the kid know? I resolved that day to make sure that Dave has no opportunities to figure out where I keep my cache of Little Debbie Nutty Bars. Or the keys to the convertible. (I do badly enough with it myself, thank you.)

Up a Tree for Christmas

Gather round, O my little sweeties, and I will tell you a Christmas story.

Yes, it's been a while since Christmas, but that doesn't mean there isn't a little mileage still to be wrung out of last year's holiday.

I should explain, as Hans Jewish Andersen, that it is only by dint of my relatively recent marriage that I have encountered some facets of this holiday up close.

In my many years on this planet, I have, of course, seen a lot of Christmas trees. But I've never had one in my house. And I'd certainly never bought one.

That latter fact must have stuck out all over me when I approached the guy in the Christmas tree lot. My wife had been planning to buy a tree the previous weekend, but her father got sick and now was in the hospital.

I thought, what the heck, I could buy her a tree. The surprise would delight her. So I trucked on down to the nearby lot, walked up to the guy, and said, "I'd like to buy a Christmas tree."

"Sure," he said. "What kind?"

Kind? What kind of Christmas tree? I had that feeling you get when you walk into a hardware store to get one of those little thingies and you find out there's a ton of those little thingies, all different.

Trying to be helpful, I replied, "A green one, I think." I

could tell that if I had been on *Family Feud,* the cries of "Good answer!" would have been pretty halfhearted.

"OK, what kinds are there?" I asked. As might surprise others who have allowed someone else—or some other population group—to buy the Christmas tree, it turns out there are many kinds, not even counting "short, "skinny" and "funnylooking." The guy, speaking rather slowly, as if to a simple child who had lost the note from his mom, asked if I wanted a long-needle tree or a short-needle tree.

Now, although my memory for facts is OK and my memory for voices and sounds is excellent, my memory for things visual is almost nonexistent. In fact, if I don't glance down I can't say what I'm wearing.

Oh, my gosh! Excuse me a minute!

There. That's better. Anyway, I certainly didn't remember what kind of Christmas tree my wife had purchased for herself before our marriage.

But I did know, based on knowing lots of her other habits, that—whatever kind she buys—she has always bought that kind, and her parents always bought that kind, and that is the only kind that really feels like Christmas, and all other kinds are very wrong. So it was important.

At my request the guy showed me a long-needle tree and a short-needle tree, staring at me the whole time as if I was from *way* outstate. The needle-length contrast was obvious, thank goodness, and it proved an ample jog to my memory: With absolutely no doubt, my wife had been buying Christmas trees that were some kind of short-needle variety. But which?

With surliness that increased with my confusion, he dragged up several short-needle trees, none of which I could tell apart, even when held right next to each other. "This is your blue spruce. See how it's different from your balsam?" No.

I think there really isn't any difference. I think these are all the same tree, marketed through General Motors, which invented calling the same car the Pontiac Grand Prix, the Oldsmobile Cutlass Supreme and the Buick Regal. But if there was a difference, and I chose wrong, I knew my wife would be able to tell from 50 yards away.

I poked and sniffed at trees, while the guy stamped his feet and blew his nose and generally tried to look as if his death from exposure was minutes away. Finally, in desperation, I announced that I wanted a blue spruce, and that since I didn't know a good one from a bad one (or from a balsam), I needed his help to get one my wife wouldn't hate. I said he could charge me extra.

"We just charge by the foot," he said. "Here's a nice one," indicating a tree whose trunk took off at a forty-five-degree angle halfway up.

"No," I said, "that one's pretty crooked. I want a really nice tree."

"How about this one? This one's real nice." The entire left half was missing for the first two feet.

"Or this one? This one's nice, too." It had a gaping hole halfway up.

Suddenly he produced what seemed to be a perfect tree. "How about this one? This one's nice."

"Fine," I said. "I'll take it." It cost an amazing amount (but, as I believe I've indicated, I'd never bought one before). While I was paying for it, he put it in my truck, which was decent of him, so I tipped him. I got that "you're from outer space" look again, so now I know that you don't tip Christmas tree guys.

Anyway, I got it home and set it up in the window. I was surprised that it dropped needles on the floor, but I swept them up and went to walk the dog. I was surprised that there were more needles on the floor when I came back, but as I believe I have pointed out, I hadn't dealt with Christmas trees before, and I assumed they did lots I didn't know about. Like maybe they snored.

I swept up again and set about doing other things. Several hours later, I heard the dog barking, signaling my wife's return. Her car was in the driveway, but she hadn't come in. She was just looking at the tree through the window. Good, I thought. I got it right.

Soon she came in, a little misty, and thanked me. "It's lovely," she said.

I was really proud of myself. So I pushed it. The Greeks call it hubris.

"I didn't know there were so many kinds of Christmas trees," I said. I heard her hesitate. And I knew. "It isn't the right kind, is it?"

"I never would have told you," she said. "It was such a nice thought."

"It was supposed to be a balsam, huh? There were three kinds of short-needle trees, and I couldn't tell the difference, but I was pretty sure the color on this one was right. At least I knew it's supposed to be a short-needle tree."

"Ummm," she said. "It's lovely, and you're a sweet person, but I always get a long-needle tree."

"Really? Gee, I'm sorry. But I was real sure. That's the only part I was sure of. And I suppose your family has always had long-needle trees and this just isn't right, huh?"

"No. In fact, my parents had trees like this one, but I didn't like them, so I switched when I got my own apartment. But it's not important; it's still a Christmas tree. And this one is very pretty." She glanced down at the floor. "It has dropped a few needles, though. You have to sweep after you set them up."

"I did. Twice."

"They saw you coming, sweetie."

Later, after most of the needles had hit the floor, we discovered that the tree contained a bird's nest, which is supposed to mean that we're going to have good luck. Or maybe, if the birds who built the nest were sick, we're going to come down with psittacosis.

Hanukkah isn't this hard.

On the Cutting Edge of Economics

ⲧⲧⲧ

As a humor columnist, I usually don't deal with economic analysis—it's too easy a target. But once in a while the complexity of a particular economic issue compels me to offer readers a more simpleminded approach than is available elsewhere.

(Think nothing of it; it comes naturally to me.)

You may have noticed that the chairman of the Federal Reserve Board, fun-loving Alan Greenspan, has been criticized by a number of equally fun-loving private economic analysts lately for cranking up interest rates to fight inflation when, they say, there doesn't seem to be any inflation. There's no rush of spending that could drive up prices, they say; just a modest recovery that leaves plenty of folks with nothing at all to spend, and isn't that just peachy?

(Economic analysts are folks who think unemployment is good because it keeps inflation down. If one of them moves into your neighborhood, put your house on the market.)

How can one account for the divergence of views between Greenspan and the others?

- (Unlikely): There's an honest difference of opinion.
- (Probable): The analysts have bet that interest rates would stay low, using money that belongs to their brothers-in-law, union pension funds and some muscular guys named Eddie. And now they're sweating

because Greenspan's rising interest rates are sending these investments down the tube.

- (Barely possible): Greenspan knows something about consumer demand that these analysts don't.

A recent experience of mine lends some credibility to the third hypothesis: It might be that, like me, Greenspan suffered this year from a bout of the unusually debilitating flu that has been going around, and that that experience, not shared by private economists (whose offices have better temperature control), has colored his outlook.

Return with me now to a time a few weeks ago, just before the flu bug hit me. I had been vaguely planning to repair a dripping pipe in my basement laundry room. It was an L-shaped piece of kitchen sink drainpipe, and it had been dripping, very slowly, for a long time. I had placed a plastic bucket under it, so in the grand scheme of things the repair was nothing urgent, but it bugged me to step around that bucket whenever I went to wash clothes.

The repair I planned was simple: Remove the leaky cast-iron pipe and replace it with inexpensive, easy-to-handle plastic drainpipe. Little rubber coupling sections with clamps would join the new pipe to stubs of the old pipe that I would leave at its ends. The whole thing would be a breeze.

Anyone who has ever done anything involving replacing existing hardware or plumbing knows that this is a piece of self-delusion: Some basic and inviolable rule of nature—perhaps it's the Fourth Law of Thermodynamics—states that any such project, no matter how apparently simple, will ultimately require three trips to the hardware store.

Beyond that consideration, which is always there—like

death, taxes and the long-distance access charge—what was keeping me from undertaking the plumbing job was the thought of cutting through the large, thick pipe to remove the leaky section. I had a clear, but unappealing, mental picture of several hours in the company of a hacksaw, followed by many days with my wrists in warm Epsom salts.

Then I got the flu. Bone-achy, dog-tired and sometimes near-delirious, I spent four days on my back staring at the TV, barely able to tell the personal-injury attorney ads from the hair-replacement ads. Not once in all the time I was really ill did I give even a moment's thought to the dripping pipe.

Then, just as suddenly as the flu had hit, it relented. Not all the way: I was still sick, but the fever broke, I was hungry and I felt strangely energized.

And the first thing I did after taking a shower, putting on real clothes and eating a couple of curiously nutritious Little Debbie Nutty Bars, was to head for the hardware store to buy some plastic drainpipe. (And a plastic-pipe elbow joint, some plastic-pipe pre-glue and plastic-pipe glue, and—foolishly trying to subvert the Fourth Law—several types of rubber coupling sections and several kinds of clamps so I wouldn't have to return to the store right away if I bought the wrong kind.)

Then, as if inspired to succeed, I did something I never do—I asked for advice. I found a hardware guy and asked him how somebody who didn't have all day managed to cut through old cast-iron drainpipe.

"With a Sawzall," he said. That turned out to be the brand name of what is generically called a reciprocating saw: a very large, mean-looking version of an electric saber saw. A saber saw with a glandular condition. A saber saw that looks as if it should be included in the crime bill.

I strolled over to the Sawzall department and determined that they ran $100 and more. At this point I would normally have gone home, looked into borrowing or renting a reciprocating saw, and no doubt spent several hours in the company of a hacksaw, followed by many days with my wrists in warm Epsom salts.

Instead, buoyed by whatever mysterious force accompanied this stage of my flu (and by my ability to spell "buoyed"), I unblinkingly bought a $105 reciprocating saw, for which I had no conceivable use beyond cutting one lousy pipe in my basement.

I went home and collapsed. A few hours later, however, I arose reenergized and descended to the basement, where, accompanied by a deafening racket, I cut through the old pipe as if it were butter.

After a few minutes of cutting the plastic pipe into two lengths, assembling it and the elbow into an "L" and installing the couplers, I was done. Or I would have been, except that I had mismeasured one leg so the new pipe was too short. Back to the hardware store for a new length of plastic pipe and a new elbow. Yes, I could have bought just a plastic sleeve and glued the old pipe and just a little extra section of leftover pipe into it. I didn't.

Back home again, I cut the new pipe more carefully, glued it together and slipped it into the two couplers that were already clamped to the ends of the old pipe. Bingo.

Except, I discovered, cutting the old pipe had further damaged a weak spot in one of the ends of it that I had left in place, and that section was now leaking.

No problem. Just cut off that weak section and . . . Of course, the newest plastic section would now be too short again and need to be replaced with one a little longer. The plastic-sleeve option sounded better, but I didn't have one, and since I would have to go back to the hardware store for that, I decided to go for the whole new pipe and elbow again. (No adding a patch to the patch for me—especially when I'm euphoric from partial flu recovery.) So back to the hardware store for the third time, thus satisfying the laws of physics.

I went home, cut off more of the old pipe and assembled and installed the new, longer replacement. Perfect! And it didn't leak.

Total cost was about $140 plus gas, but besides a non-leaking pipe I now have a really frightening power tool that I'll never use again. And a gaping hole in my checkbook.

That brings me back to my main point: Had I not caught the flu and more or less lost my mind, I wouldn't have spent $105 on a reciprocating saw—and I probably would have put off the rest of the $35 repair as well.

If mine is a typical response to this flu, and all over the country people are buying reciprocating saws, Mustang convertibles or egg beaters that they only need once or twice and can't really afford, Greenspan might be correct.

In that case, I have only three pieces of advice: Rest in bed, drink plenty of fluids and lock up your checkbook until you—or the economy—have fully recovered.

What a Tangled Web We Weave

ͳͳͳ

Of the many invaluable aspects of the Internet, the one Uncle Al invalues most is that it gives us much greater access to misinformation.

Not long ago you had to do some work to expose yourself to rumors, ill-informed medical advice, insistently bad spelling (where would you have seen "ware and tare" if not for eBay?) and incorrect "facts." All of that now comes to you with the click of a button.

And if, back then, you started to look for some information but you had the principal word misspelled, you couldn't get very far until you realized that. No longer; now you can learn from people who are just as misinformed as you.

The other day Uncle Al heard a swell new word describing a tiny sliver of this wonderful world of error, in connection with "cyber-squatters"—people who registered Web sites with names of big companies or famous people who hadn't gotten around to starting Web sites for themselves. The squatters then tried to sell the sites to the companies or celebrities for lots of money.

(If, for example, you had registered www.UncleAl.com, and Uncle Al was famous and decided he cared—which he isn't and doesn't—you might have tried to make him buy the name from you.)

What Uncle Al just heard about is a tiny part of cyber-squatting: registering *incorrect* Web site names. Kevin Spacey recently got a ruling against someone who had registered www.kevinspacy.com—which isn't how he spells his name, but lots of people don't know that. This practice is called "typo squatting."

Although people visiting a typo squatter's site probably don't know its name is misspelled (they got there in the first place because they couldn't spell it), the typo squatter probably does. A more common Internet phenomenon is acquiring "knowledge" from people who *don't* know they're wrong.

There are more entries on the Web for "German Chocolate Cake" than for "German's Chocolate Cake." Although the recipe was born in Texas and popularized by the maker of one of its ingredients (German's Sweet Chocolate, a product named for its founder, Sam German), most people apparently think it's a German cake recipe, and that's how they spell it.

Comparatively recently, search engines began suggesting alternate spellings. (If you look for "Steven King" you'll get the many misspelled entries but you will also be asked "Did you mean: *Stephen King*?") Unfortunately, these suggestions aren't based on which spelling is correct, but partly on which is more common on the Web. So when you search for "German's Chocolate Cake," you fastidious speller, you will be greeted by the annoying "Did you mean: *German* Chocolate Cake?"

Another large chunk of the misinformation on the Internet is in e-mail: urban legends (Neiman Marcus did not charge anyone $250 for a cookie recipe), outright junk (myriad get-rich-quick proposals), and a whole raft of stuff (missing kids, product recalls, contest rules) each item of which was perfectly true when Adam told Eve but wasn't by the time umpteen thousand people had e-mailed it to each other and, years later, it finally got to you.

Misinformation is everywhere, of course, not just on the Web, and people who have "facts," however wrong they are, like to cling to them.

Uncle Al, whose last name, incidentally, is pronounced "SICK-er-man," loves a story from his son Dave, who while in college in North Carolina met a kid from Minneapolis.

"My dad writes for the paper there," Dave said.

"Oh? What's his name?"

"Al Sicherman."

"I thought it was pronounced 'SISH-er-man.'"

"No, it's 'SICK-er-man.'"

"Are you sure?"

But Uncle Al's current favorite peculiar "fact" is from the Web, and its peculiarity results from his failure to identify the source. That was an omission almost impossible to make in the dim past, when one first selected a reference book and then found the fact within it, instead of finding the fact and possibly noting—but probably not—who or what was its source.

(Sidestepping the whole question of information source was, in effect, the point of the entertainment activity referred to as "just surfing the Web." Web surfing seems to have been a phase, and it appears no longer to be much more popular than the cellulose equivalent—spending hours in the library looking at random pages of books chosen by spine color.)

Anyway, Uncle Al and a colleague were discussing people's overreaction to increased gasoline prices. They agreed that it's one thing for truckers to talk about gas prices ruining them, and that conservation is good, but it's pretty hilarious when people say they're rethinking a 600-mile driving vacation because they'd be pouring all their money into the gas tank.

Uncle Al calculated that an extra 50 cents a gallon, in a car that gets 20 miles to the gallon, would make a 600-mile trip cost $15 more—surely not enough to blow a vacation out of the water unless it was going to be a pretty lousy vacation anyway. (This is going somewhere. Hang on.)

Uncle Al noted that he plans to drive to New York to visit Dave, and that high gas prices weren't making him consider staying home. He decided to do that cost calculation for his trip, but he didn't know offhand how far New York is from Minneapolis.

So, because the Internet is just a click away on his computer, he typed "mileage between cities" into a search engine, which found many mileage calculators. He clicked on the first one, which displayed two boxes: "from" and "to."

He clicked on the "from" box, clicked Minneapolis on the list that opened up, then clicked on the "to" box. New York wasn't in the list displayed there, but . . . ah! Manhattan was. Strange, but lots of things are strange. He clicked Manhattan, and then the "Find Mileage" button.

The answer was 77 miles.

Had it said 1,152 miles, or 2,273, Uncle Al probably would have believed it, and he would have gone on to base his gas calculation—and maybe the rest of his life—on that number. As it was, he burst out laughing, then looked more closely at the "mileage calculator" site.

It was from the Kansas Department of Transportation.

The good part about a 77-mile trip from Minneapolis, Kansas, to Manhattan, Kansas, is that it's so short that Uncle Al wouldn't even have to consider, as part of his car costs, the effects of ware and tare.

How Much Is in the Glass?

The other morning, Uncle Al was reading an analysis of one or another of the world's current collection of horrible situations, in order to get an early start on ruining his day, only to find the whole mess summed up with that thing about the optimist seeing the glass half full and the pessimist seeing it half empty.

Uncle Al found this quite annoying, not only because he is easily annoyed (although he is), nor even because he could have written that himself even if he didn't know anything about the situation (and in fact, when he was done reading, he still didn't know anything about it).

Mostly Uncle Al found this annoying because he knows that the world consists of zillions of interest groups—not just optimists and pessimists—so the glass-half-full/glass-half-empty analysis utterly misrepresents the incredible panoply of possible views.

Following is the merest sample of how others might explain or describe a half-empty/half-full glass of water:

- High-school science teacher: The glass contains 4 ounces of water.
- Statistician: There's a 95 percent probability that the glass contains between 3½ and 4½ ounces of water.
- Minnesota Twins: That's the last water you get

unless you replace that crummy old glass with a brand-new one—with gold trim.

- Minnesota Vikings: Actually, you need to replace that crummy old glass with two brand-new glasses—one with gold trim and one with platinum. Each will be one-quarter full—or three-quarters empty.

- Liberal legislator: This isn't enough water. To meet the community's needs, each of us needs to add more water.

- Conservative legislator: We don't need to find more water; we're already putting in way too much water. What we need is a smaller glass.

- Governor Ventura: You know, I just might close the kitchen altogether.

- Enron: You don't actually have half a glass of water: Bottom line, you owe other people 17½ glasses of water, but we kept track of those partnerships "off the books." And we're shredding the glass.

- Bill Clinton: Never mind the water: That's one very attractive glass!

- Alexander Haig: I'm in charge of this glass of water.

- Microsoft: The use of water isn't fully supported in Glass 95, Glass 98 or Glass 2000; you need to upgrade to Glass XP. If that doesn't fill the glass, it's a hardware problem.

- Intel: This kind of thing works better with a Pentium 4 chip, but it's basically a software problem.

- Apple: Why put the water in a glass? That isn't necessary on our platform.

- Dear Abby: You deserve more, honey. Dump that glass!
- Psychologist: How does half a glass of water make you feel?
- Psychiatrist: In some cases of water/glass anxiety, selective serotonin reuptake inhibitors such as Prozac have been found to be helpful.
- Surgeon: We're going to have to remove half of your glass.
- Chiropractor: OK, hold still—I'm going to adjust your glass.
- Dentist: There's a hole in the glass; the only chance to save it is to drill all the way down through the table.
- Airline: We seem to have misplaced your glass. Oh—and the water, too. Would you like some pretzels?
- Plumber: I was afraid of this: You're going to need a whole new glass—and if you want me to replace it right now, it's going to cost you double time on the labor.
- Attorney: I think you have a good chance of winning the other half of the water in a lawsuit. I'll take only 25 percent of all of it.
- Economist: The index of future intentions of water-purchasing managers is down, but inventories of water are steady and the salty-snack index is at a three-month high. So it's not too clear how much of the water we're seeing is really in the glass right now and how much is water we expect to be there.
- Palestinian: It's our water. Give us more water or

we'll break the glass. Then neither of us will be able to drink, and that will teach you!

- Israeli: It's our water. You can't have more water; we gave you some water and now you want even more water. We're going to shut off all the water. Then neither of us will be able to drink, and that will teach you!

- TV news teaser: Something is terribly wrong with your glass of water. We'll tell you what at 10.

- Newspaper article: Water glass stands at 50 percent/ Views differed sharply at marches and rallies around the Twin Cities Sunday on the relative merits of half a glass of water. But there was wide agreement that the matter must be resolved so that the Legislature can proceed to a vote on a bill to lift a ban on proposed enforcement of a moratorium on the passage of limits on rule-making proposals.

- *Discover* magazine article: HALF: Full/Empty? The antecedents of this contentious topic go back hundreds—if not thousands—of years, well before there was anything we would recognize as a glass. Delbert Dull, deputy assistant director of the Institute for Advanced Study of Recessed Objects, points to cave paintings in France that . . .

- TV reporter: Everyone needs water. So you know what it looks like, I'm standing in front of a lake. And now here's film of people drinking water somewhere. But soon you might not be able to drink so much water. Little Billy Smith of Bloomington doesn't like that idea one bit. "Do you think you'll like having half a glass of water, Billy?" "No." "Why

not?" "Uhhh." "Do you like water, Billy?" "Yes."
"There you have it. Back to you, Paul."

- Auto mechanic: Oh, man! Some idiot installed the wrong glass!
- Auto dealer: All the glasses of water are like that now.

Voyager's Message to the Stars

ᗰᗰᗰ

As the *Voyager 2* spacecraft heads out of the solar system, scientists tell us that in 6,582 years it will pass within 4.03 light-years of Barnard's Star, which is said to have a planet. That might seem to raise some pretty exciting possibilities for contact with another civilization.

Unfortunately, a dramatic encounter between *Voyager 2* and residents of the planet of Barnard's Star is not very likely.

First of all, although *Voyager* will come within 4.03 light-years of Barnard's Star, that's still two-thirds of the 6-light-year distance from here to Barnard's Star in the first place. So if you stay up late to watch it on TV in the year 8571,* bear in mind that 4.03 light-years (23.7 trillion miles) won't exactly be a close pass.

(*Actually, you'll have to stay up late in the year 8575, because although the flyby will occur in 8571 it will take 4.03 years for the TV signal to reach here at the speed of light. And you might not get to see it anyway, because the Barnard's Star coverage might not preempt reruns of *The Lucy Show*.)

To pound home the point (you're welcome), the distance of 23.7 trillion miles that will remain between *Voyager* and Barnard's Star at *Voyager*'s closest approach is about 6,400 times the distance from the sun to Pluto. Or, in plainer terms, at 650 miles per hour in a fast commercial jet, it's a trip of 4.2 million years.

And even if somehow they take such immense distances in stride, it isn't real likely that the Bleebnoids on Barnard's Planet will come out 23.7 trillion miles to have a look at *Voyager* as it tootles by, because it is very unlikely that they'll know it's there. It isn't exactly huge, after all. It weighs 1,819 pounds, about as much as the average Holstein cow, so it will be relatively hard to detect from a distance of 23.7 trillion miles.

OK, it is possible that the Bleebnoids wouldn't all be sitting on Barnard's Planet whistling "Blarglk" (a secessionist anthem from an ancient period of unrest). Conceivably some of them might be out joyriding 23.7 trillion miles from home.

(Parents: It's 8571. Do you know where your flying saucer is?)

If that's the case, they might indeed encounter *Voyager* on its lonely trip through the interstellar void. And what would they find if they did? Well, believe it or not, *Voyager* mission scientists tell us they would find on the side of the spacecraft a twelve-inch gold-plated copper disc of recorded sounds from Earth, as well as a cartridge, needle, and instructions, in a scientific code, as to how to play it. Swell, huh? The sounds include greetings in 35 languages, a clap of thunder, frogs croaking, a baby's cry and Chuck Berry singing "Johnny B. Goode."

OK, imagine you're a Bleebnoid, or perhaps a Blarglkian or even a passerby from Deneb. Assuming you're up on decoding scientific codes (maybe you're wearing your Scientific Decoder Ring) and that you can actually pick up the cartridge and needle and play the record (that you aren't merely an intelligent gas cloud or an astral projection or a nightmare from a corned-beef sandwich), and that you have at least one ear and that you choose to play the disc someplace where there's an atmosphere so that you can hear it—assuming all that, what would you make of the recording?

I'm only guessing, here, not being an alien being, but surely the creatures who discover Voyager would assume that the message at the beginning is one long communication, not the same thing in 35 different languages. (Would you expect a message from the planet Twylo to be in 35 different Twylian languages?) This means that they will have some difficulty in translating it.

One has to wonder about the point of the 35-language message. Did we think maybe there's somebody in deep space who speaks French?

Anyway, moving along, now picture the poor Bleebnoid hunched over the disc, spinning it with six or seven appendages while holding the cartridge and needle with another, when suddenly, after endless babble, there is a clap of thunder. Startling, at the least. Especially if it's in stereo. Probably made him drop the cartridge and his copy of *How to Decode Scientific Code*. There seems no question but that an intelligent being would take the crash of thunder as a threat, following whatever warning is contained in the opening message.

So far, then, we have *"Guten tag bonjour jo napot ohhayoh gohzaymas marhaba buenas dias* [and so on], *BOOM."* Next come "Ribbit, ribbit" and "Waaah!" Possibly those are recognizable as not more of the first message. (But possibly not, too. Just because he's 23.7 trillion miles from Barnard's Star, our Bleebnoid ain't necessarily no rocket scientist. Maybe that was his momma.) But if he does figure out that the frog and baby noises are not another version of *buon giorno,* what would he think they mean?

Your guess on what an alien who's just heard greetings in 35 languages would make of frogs is as good as mine, but if evolution on Barnard's Planet or wherever ran remotely like it did on Earth, the baby's cry might be recognized at least as something in pain. So the thoughtful six-eyed slime-borer could well take it as more of the *BOOM* warning.

Finally, "Johnny B. Goode." Who on Earth picked this stuff? Everything else aside, I'd be willing to bet that at least 99 percent of the people on *this* planet think that the song's title is "Johnny Be Good." And what meaning is even the most perceptive ammonia-breathing lizard-buffalo supposed to attach to this?:

"Go! Go! Go! Johnny! Go! Go! Go! Johnny! Go! Go! Go! Johnny! Go! Go! Go! Johnny! Go! Go! Johnny B. Goode."

All I can say is that the next time we launch a deep-space probe, I hope they ask me what to put on the side of it, so that we can let the universe know easily and clearly what our civilization is really about: Zap-a-Pack microwaveable Cheez Whiz.

The Joke That Never Fails

᠆ᠭᠭᠭ

America's foremost philosopher, Mel Brooks, has observed, "We mock the thing we are to be." If so, Uncle Al must assume that in his own youth he mocked older people's forgetfulness. Because now he can't remember what he mocked.

Uncle Al's spotty memory was the subject of a recent phone conversation with his son Dave, who had called because he was telling a friend about Uncle Al's plan to post a joke outside the door to his room in The Home—but Dave couldn't remember (the problem apparently starts early) what joke Uncle Al had chosen.

Uncle Al will make his explanation brief because he knows he has discussed this topic previously with about 400,000 of his closest friends. He comes by that certainty not because he remembers having discussed this here before (he doesn't, and in fact he would have bet against it), but because he just looked it up.

So, a quick review: Uncle Al knows that when he is in The Home he will enjoy hearing a joke from his visitors, some of whom might not have a joke to tell him, so he plans to have one posted at his door.

Sure, he will be hearing the same joke from every visitor every time, but that's no problem because Uncle Al will, of course, forget the joke as soon as he's heard it. But that doesn't mean it can be just any joke—it should be a joke that he identifies now as one he really likes, to ensure that it will be a hit when visitors toss it at him in The Home.

For that reason, and because he vaguely remembers having done so, Uncle Al is quite sure he picked out the joke for his door many years ago. But—as of late 1997, when he last discussed this in print—he had (surprise!) forgotten what it was, and he had settled on another one, at least until he came up with the first one or something better.

So that second choice is the joke he told Dave. Here it is:

"My dog has no nose." "How does he smell?" "Terrible."

That's it: You're on and you're off, presumably leaving Uncle Al laughing.

Dave, perhaps with some lingering memory of the first joke Uncle Al had selected, was not at all satisfied.

"That's it?" he complained. "That's no good. It takes two people to tell it. What if I visit you by myself?"

Uncle Al was so nonplussed he whizzed past minused and wound up somewhere in the middle of long-divisioned.

"I don't see the problem," he expostulated. (Uncle Al enjoys expostulating, because it sends many people to their dictionaries.) "You just tell it, bang-bang-bang, like Henny Youngman: '"Doctor, Doctor! Nobody pays any attention to me!" Doctor says "Next!"' Or '"Doctor, Doctor! The Invisible Man is here." "Tell him I can't see him!"'"

(Uncle Al modestly draws your attention to the quotation marks within quotation marks within quotation marks, rarely seen these days except in accounts of joke telling. He would have gone one level deeper, having the receptionist quote the Invisible Man saying, "I've been waiting almost an hour," for example, but he didn't want to show off.)

Dave remained unsatisfied, so Uncle Al suggested that, for any visitor somehow not comfortable with that one-person joke-telling arrangement, a note could be posted next to the joke. Something like this:

"Do you need a second person to assist you in telling this joke? If you go down the hall to the office, somebody there can help."

As those words escaped his lips, Uncle Al realized that he had just set up a story that a friend had told him some years ago. He has retold it so often himself that he classifies it as one of his hands-on-buzzer stories. (When an obvious occasion for telling it arises, he invites those present to stop him by making a buzzing noise if they've heard it. If even one person in the group doesn't buzz, he gets to tell it again.)

So sure was Uncle Al that he had told it many times to Dave or in his presence that he waited for Dave to buzz, or perhaps to chime in with the punch line.

When that didn't happen, Uncle Al began to feel his universe shifting. Had he really never told Dave this story? It seemed impossible that he could have forgotten or misremembered something associated with his deepest, most basic core value: making sure, by frequent repetition, that his son knows all his stories by heart. Still . . .

Was Uncle Al, in fact, slipping so badly that he was already standing at the figurative door of The Home?

His voice quavering a bit, Uncle Al began to tell Dave the story: A well-known local musician, a little full of himself, was part of a group playing a benefit concert at a nursing home. As he walked down the corridor, nodding or saying "hello" to residents, an elderly man said "hello" back. The musician stopped, turned to him and said, "Do you know who I am?"

"No," the man replied, "but . . ." and here, much to Uncle Al's relief (and probably to Dave's, too), Dave chimed in: "If you go down the hall to the office, somebody there can tell you."

Uncle Al continued to feel much better through the subsequent conversation until he realized that he couldn't remember why he had called Dave in the first place.

Underneath It All, a Loss

᠀᠀᠀

Life provides us all with embarrassing moments. (So do *Time* and *Sports Illustrated,* but not quite as often.) A lunch conversation with some colleagues not long ago produced several stories of chagrin with one central theme—a theme that, it turns out, has also appeared in the life of one of my relatives.

I pass these stories along for entertainment purposes only. The names have been changed, to protect the innocent.

The theme today, friends, is underwear loss, and the heartbreak associated therewith. Perhaps you have never experienced this humiliating phenomenon. Or perhaps, like one colleague who recalled her own tragedy from something like third grade, it is a fairly remote memory. (The elastic was loose; they fell off on the way home. Nobody saw it happen, but she was mortified.)

But maybe, like two people I've heard about, something of the kind happened to you in adulthood.

Here is One Person's Sad Story:

Prudence (not her real name) and her sister were on a vacation a few years ago in Fort Lauderdale, Florida (not a real city). One night they got back to their hotel late and very tired. Prudence got undressed hurriedly and climbed into bed, leaving her clothes in a heap.

Next morning, when Prudence arose refreshed and put on her jeans again, she didn't notice that the previous day's underwear had remained bunched up inside. She and her sister had breakfast and set out to gawk at the shops on one of the area's most exclusive and expensive streets.

The weather as they strolled was so gorgeous and the whole experience so exhilarating that, despite the posh neighborhood, Prudence just couldn't restrain herself from doing a high kick.

And her underwear came shooting out of her pants leg.

And here is My Relative's Tale:

Cousin Daisy (not her real name, not our real relationship) had a particularly busy day one wintry weekend a few years ago. She went to a garage sale, then to a wedding, and then shopping at an antique store with a girlfriend. This necessitated two changes of clothes: from casual weekend wear to fancy clothes and back.

Being that kind of person, Daisy put on new underwear when she changed into the dress for the wedding. When she got back home to change back into her jeans to go antiquing, she failed to notice that (yes) the morning underwear remained bunched up in the jeans.

Later that afternoon, as she and her girlfriend maneuvered a newly purchased old table from the antique store to their car, being careful to avoid setting it down in the slush, Daisy's friend noticed a pair of underpants in the gutter. The two wondered aloud, with much smirking, what kind of person, in what circumstances, would wind up losing her underwear in the gutter.

Suddenly Daisy's girlfriend said, "Those look like the underpants I gave you for Christmas."

To which Daisy replied, "They sure do. My goodness! They *are* mine!"

If this particular disaster has happened to two adults in my small circle of friends and relatives, to how many millions—or billions—more might it also have occurred? Could it be one of the many unpleasant phenomena that social scientists say are underreported?

Surely it has happened to men as well as to women, but men might be even less likely to discuss it. Would the executive secretary of the federal Bureau of Missing Undergarments advise that for every incident of adult underwear loss we hear about at least twenty are never reported?

What conclusions might we draw?

Well, let's not be negative. Why not turn this problem into an opportunity—an opportunity once and for all to restore the United States to its position of world leadership in technology?

We have already lost the VCR, and it may be too late to hang onto high-definition TV and supercomputers, but there's still time to beat Japan in directing our industrial and technical prowess toward designing a device that sets off a warning when it detects underwear bunched up inside your jeans:

A shorts circuit.

Credit Where Credit Is Due

For many years Uncle Al was able to manage his life very nicely without credit cards. If he saw something he wanted or needed to buy, and he didn't have the required amount of money in his checking account, he didn't buy whatever it was until he did.

If it appeared that the opportunity to own an exquisite porcelain doll of a child eating his first Big Mac, for example, might elude his grasp because he was temporarily short of funds, he regarded that as one of the breaks. In fact, very few things got away from him simply because he waited until he had the money. Often, in fact, he decided that the hamburger doll (or whatever) was cheesy, and he didn't buy it at all.

Then one day, a trigger in Uncle Al's brain silently went off. Suddenly, what had long been joyously obvious to others became clear to him:

If he encountered something that was expensive, so that he wouldn't be able to pay for it next payday either, he could save up for the purchase every month and buy it 18 months later—or he could charge it now and pay back for the purchase over the next 18 months. That way, he would have the object now, instead of 18 months later. The only difference would be the interest— and even at fairly steep rates, the total extra outlay for interest wasn't very much.

How had he misunderstood this for so long? How many wonderful things had he failed to buy and enjoy simply in order to avoid using a credit card?

Things changed in a big way for Uncle Al. Why postpone purchase of a $180 whatsis, when it would be only $10 a month, plus a little interest, paid off over 18 months?

Thus Uncle Al acquired a whatsis, and then a frammis and then several assorted precision widgets.

Much, much later, peering out from under his pile of whatsises, frammises, widgets and debt, it became clear to Uncle Al that there was a second difference between saving up for something for 18 months and charging it now and paying for it for the next 18 months: If he was out of money it was impossible to save up for more things; but being out of money didn't stop him from putting more things on his charge card.

Soon it became clear that something had to change. And the change turned out not to be too difficult: Uncle Al simply began thinking of the payback period for his purchases not as 18 months, but as five years. Thus the monthly payment for a $180 item went from $10 to $3 (plus a little interest).

In addition to lowering the amount Uncle Al tried to come up with every month to pay for his pile of whatsises, frammises and widgets, there was a real plus side to this revision: At only $3 a month each, Uncle Al could afford to buy quite a few more $180 whatsises, frammises and widgets.

Eventually, Uncle Al's pile of stuff was so large that although the monthly interest charge was indeed small for each, the interest payment for the whole pile of stuff was no longer small at all. It was large enough to buy one or more frammises—in cash—every month. And it wasn't buying any frammises at all.

Along about here in Uncle Al's financial saga, he began getting offers of new credit cards in the mail. Many of them had very low introductory interest rates for as much as a year, and some of those offered free balance transfers from existing charge cards.

Over several years, Uncle Al opened many new accounts, and transferred many balances from previous accounts, and as soon as the low interest rates on those new accounts expired, he transferred the balances to still-newer accounts with low rates.

Also, of course, he bought the occasional widget or frammis—hey, he was paying only 5.9 percent on the balance; he could afford an indulgence now and then.

At one point, Uncle Al had as many as a dozen cards with active balances. Although most were at quite low interest rates, the total of all the minimum monthly payments was beginning to cut into his purchase of Little Debbie snack cakes. Things had gotten out of hand.

Uncle Al finally consolidated all those credit card balances in a home-equity loan, and is having the payment for that loan deducted from his paycheck. Whew. And he is now fully convinced that he can't afford any more whatsises, frammises or widgets. End of story.

Sort of.

Uncle Al has been manfully resisting offers in the mail of preapproved credit cards with low introductory interest rates. It hasn't been difficult; Uncle Al already has many credit cards he's not using, and he knows better—maybe—than to get into that whole thing again.

He also is resisting the blank cash-advance checks sent to him by the purveyors of the credit cards he already has. "Need cash for home repairs? Vacations? Whatsises and frammises? Just write out this check and the money is yours." It's easier to resist these because the danger of writing a big fat check is so clear.

And he is resisting even more easily the really frightening new tack by credit card and loan companies—those with which he has accounts and those he's never gone near—to send him fully made-out checks for large amounts. (Cash it and it's a cash advance charged to your account, or a loan.)

The issuer of a credit card he's not using sent him such a check for $3,000 a few weeks ago. A bank with which he has never dealt sent him such a check for $7,500, and after he ignored it (actually, after he ripped it up, saying several curses over it and flushing it down the toilet), they sent him another one with a note that began, "Perhaps you missed our Signet Instant Loan offer the first time."

The most farfetched one was a check for $2,544.50 (maybe they know something about what Uncle Al ought to buy) from a local loan office, written on a Delaware bank of the same name. There's a $25 fee, which isn't bad as these things go; the transaction is described as a loan, not a cash advance, and the annual interest rate is—wait for it—26.35 percent! (Paid off in 36 installments of $103 each, the total finance charge is $1,163.50!)

Uncle Al figured that was about as cheesy as these things could get. Then he started receiving small pieces of paper from the companies that issued some of his credit cards. They were headed "IMPORTANT NOTICE" and were full of tiny, tiny type outlining changes in the "cardholder agreement." Most seemed to concern increases in fees (late fees, cash advance fees, over-limit fees, and so on) and interest rates. They would have been pretty scary to him if he were still using the cards.

(A warning, then, to all of Uncle Al's cardholder friends: If you're using the cards, read those notices. Lots of the late-payment and over-limit fees have gone up to $25.)

Last week, however, he got what he thinks is the crowning achievement of the credit card companies, especially now that he has—he hopes—shaken off the why-not-charge-it syndrome. He got one of those tiny type "IMPORTANT NOTICE" leaflets from a card he has stopped using, and he was skimming it as he held it above the wastebasket (only because the TV show he was watching had broken for commercials):

Yadda, yadda, yadda. Late fee goes to $25. Yadda, yadda, yadda. Over-limit fee, $25. Yadda, yadda, yadda. Returned-check fee, $25. What does Uncle Al care? He's not using the card. Yadda, yadda . . . WHAT?

"If your account remains inactive for six consecutive billing cycles . . . we may charge a fee of $15." A fee for not using the account!

(Another warning, then, to all of Uncle Al's cardholder friends: If you're *not* using the cards, read those notices.)

Uncle Al rushed to close the account by phone, reading as he did so the next tiny type part of the "IMPORTANT NOTICE." He must resort to paraphrase, because it's wordy and confusing, but it says that if you decide to close your account, and you don't say you're doing it because of any of the changes in the "cardholder agreement," they can charge you $25 to close the account!

(A final warning, then, to all of Uncle Al's cardholder friends: Arrrgggh!)

One Man, Two Cars

In which the writer once more reveals the depths of his rigidity—and the breadth of his stupidity. Future students of the genre, please note.

I recently needed to haul some large boxes out of the basement, where they had been gathering dust for several years, and put them into storage elsewhere. Never mind wondering why; today's opus will be sufficiently complex without further details on that score.

The easiest route for such a box-moving operation was up the basement stairs, through the door on the landing and out into the garage, whence the boxes could be hauled away. Going up into the house and out the front door instead would involve several more turns, as well as potential disastrous contact with the dining-room chandelier; it was never a serious possibility.

My wife was gone for the afternoon; it was a perfect time for this undertaking in case I changed my mind and lugged something through the dining room. I wouldn't enjoy her not enjoying that.

All I had to do to get going was move the convertible out of the garage. Once again (faithful readers, please yawn and skip ahead), I must explain that I have this other car. I probably spent less than half what you spent on your car for both this now-gracelessly-rusting 1971 Olds Cutlass convertible, which I drive only in the summer, and my regular transportation (an old pickup that's great for hauling stuff from point A to about halfway to point B, where I must stop to see how much oil has dripped from an unfindable leak in its rebuilt engine). I always feel that I must apologize for having two vehicles. (I'm sorry. So there.)

Anyway, it had been in the cold garage since October, and after lunch I climbed in with crossed fingers, since the battery might not hold up to very much cranking.

Wrong. *Urrrk*: The battery was already dead.

A quick check revealed that the jumper cables I had would not reach from the pickup all the way into the garage, so I'd have to get the car out of there to get it started. No problem; the garage floor is level and the driveway actually slants slightly down. A couple of good shoves ought to get it out where it . . . would roll uncontrollably down the driveway and smash into either a tree or the side of some passing vehicle.

Impressed with myself for having for once thought ahead, I positioned myself between the front of the car and the large pile of whatever it is that winds up piled in garages. I needed to give the car a shove while being prepared to pull back on it in case it moved too easily. Not the simplest thing to do, especially with a trick back.

Sproing!

The car moved about a foot and my back went out. After a 15-minute rest on the kitchen floor while the dog danced around my head because nobody is supposed to lie down on the kitchen floor except him, I went back into the garage.

The first shove left room for me to assume a more back-friendly posture for pushing, which I did very gently, both to save my back and because I was aware that I was now in no condition to stop the car if it moved too fast.

After a few minutes of nudging it, I managed to get the Olds out of the garage; I jumped the battery and started it up. I left it running outside at a fast idle to charge the battery, and went to lie down on an actual bed for a few minutes while the dog danced around my head because nobody is supposed to lie down while a car is running outside.

I had noticed that one of the Olds's tires was very soft, and as I attempted, unsuccessfully, to convince the dog that I was asleep, it occurred to me that if I drove the car to the gas 'n' goods store a little more than a mile away, to inflate the tire, I would be charging the battery as I drove. A typically smooth Al Sicherman plan.

So I got up and drove over to the store. As I pulled up next to the air hose, I saw my hand reaching for the key. Even as I thought to myself "Don't do it!" the hand shut off the key, leaving me with a car whose battery, I was quite sure, was nowhere near charged enough to start it.

Urrrk. That was correct.

I inflated the tire, kicking it and myself for my stupidity. Now I was a mile from home, it was quite a cold day and a walk that long was not exactly appealing. Muttering darkly, I called a cab to take me home so that I could get my truck to jump-start the Olds.

I must confess that neither when the Olds was stuck in the garage nor when it was stuck at the store did it occur to me to call a garage to jump-start it. I don't know what this means about me.

Waiting about half an hour for the cab, most of that time in the cold lest I miss its arrival, I realized that once I got home and came back with the truck to start the car, I would be in the position of having two vehicles to get back home, but I didn't want to think about that.

It was 3:30 when the cab showed up.

On the short ride home, I felt compelled to explain to the driver that my car wouldn't start. "So what are you going to do when you get home?" he asked.

I hate smart cabdrivers.

So I got home, drove the truck to the store, and jump-started the Olds. Then I drove the Olds two blocks, walked back and got the truck, drove it four blocks, walked back and got the Olds, drove it four blocks, walked back and got the truck, and so on. In effect, I walked home, dragging both the truck and the Olds.

As I leapfrogged the two vehicles southward, I was actually hiking northward in stages, to get to the one that was then farther back. Every leg of that hike started farther south. Not long into the whole process I encountered a guy who was walking south. A few minutes later, a little farther south, I met him again, and he looked at me with what seemed to be deep suspicion.

I would have met him a third time, but he crossed the street to avoid me.

I got home at 5:30 and went to bed.

When my wife walked in from an afternoon of shopping, she asked how the day had gone.

"Terrible," I began. "I didn't get any of the boxes out of the basement."

"Well," she said, "you're entitled to take an afternoon off once in a while."

(Concluding paragraph deleted at the request of the Society for Appropriate Language.)

Outsourcing's Circle of Cutbacks

꿍꿍ꍏ

In addition to Uncle Al's many and painfully detailed descriptions of household and automotive repairs that required multiple trips to the hardware store, he also has focused the brilliant searchlight of his powerful column on examining disturbing trends and imagining how much more disturbing they might get if it were up to morons like him—or economists.

A trend we're hearing a great deal about these days is "outsourcing"—specifically the relatively recent practice of shifting such jobs as customer-service representative to low-wage economies overseas, where the whole idea of the $79 towel-warmer you're ordering is offensive to the $5-a-day person taking your call.

In a move close to Uncle Al's figurative home—although it is literally quite distant—the Reuters news agency has moved financial reporting about some U.S. firms to India. Really. It seems that the data necessary to write the reports is on the Internet, so they can be written in India as easily as in the United States. Maybe even more easily because nobody is calling the Indian writers to urge them to switch phone companies.

Upon learning of this development, Uncle Al arranged, as an experiment, to have today's column written for $6 by a contract employee at a journalism factory in Fluoristan, a barely functioning country low in tooth decay. (The $6 was the standing price, Uncle Al learned, but until now there had been no takers.)

If this deal were to continue, Uncle Al would work 3½ days a week, doing whatever he does in the Taste section, but instead of writing and polishing this column for the other 1½ days, he'd stay home and watch reruns of *Matlock*. But without that 1½ days' pay, he would have to seriously reduce his purchases of Little Debbie Nutty Bars, mystery novels, doughnuts, chocolate, butter, cream, and bizarre collectibles.

It goes without saying that he would stop buying the newspaper. But he felt like saying it anyway.

He does not, by himself, consume enough of any of these items (possibly except Little Debbie Nutty Bars) for his cutback to affect production, but if enough other high-living columnists were to be outsourced, reduced demand might result in doughnut-industry layoffs. That might cut demand among remaining doughnut-shop employees for copies of the *National Enquirer,* and so on.

At the other end of this deal is the author of the outsourced column, who lives in Squalor (the capital of Fluoristan). Uncle Al must say that the column wasn't terrible. Here are the first three paragraphs:

> Uncle Izblk was minding his own business recently (partly because the last time he minded somebody else's business, that whole family attacked his hut with pitchforks, and it took him three days and five trips to the Pile of Dirt to repair it), when he noticed that the back of his oxcart was sagging to one side.
>
> To tell the truth (although that is not usually a good idea in Fluoristan), Uncle Izblk rather enjoys relating tales of oxcart repairs that involve multiple trips to the Pile of Rocks to find just the right rock

for beating against the end of the axle to mash it out enough that the wheel won't fall off. Uncle Izblk knows that newer oxcarts have a stick through a hole near the end of the axle to keep the wheel from falling off, but he regards keeping the wheel on the old way as a challenge.

So Uncle Izblk drank a cup of mud (he understands that in some places "mud" is slang for a caffeine beverage—that is not the case in Fluoristan) and set off for the Pile of Rocks.

Uncle Al now has mixed feelings about this project.

On one hand, he feels he earns his salary—he provides at least 98 cents' worth of effort for every dollar he is paid (once in a while he just hides in the elevator or walks around the newsroom, carrying papers and looking thoughtful). And he's not sold on the idea that jobs sent abroad turn into demand for American products.

(Heck, even if Uncle Izblk wanted to spend all $6 on Little Debbie Nutty Bars, mystery novels, and American doughnuts, chocolate, butter, cream and bizarre collectibles—which Uncle Al thinks even an economist would agree is unlikely—it's only $6, compared with the 1½ days of U.S.-scale wages that Uncle Al would stop spending on that stuff if Uncle Izblk got the job.)

On the other hand, Uncle Al realized that he's not fully comfortable saying that Uncle Izblk (who seems like a nice-enough fellow who happens to live in Fluoristan) isn't entitled to— if not a slice of the pie, at least a little bite of the pie. Or maybe just to lick the plate after Uncle Al eats the pie.

One solution would be for Uncle Izblk to sell his $6 columns to newspapers in Fluoristan (if there were any), and to spend the $6 in the Fluoristani economy, where it would buy lots more (because Fluoristan's lousy wages mean stuff produced there is cheap). All that's needed to get that ball rolling is to jump-start the Fluoristani economy. (But if anybody here knew how to do that, Uncle Al wishes they'd jump-start this one first.)

Or perhaps Fluoristani workers should organize and demand better wages. Higher wages in Fluoristan would reduce the advantage of outsourcing—and the better wages for any jobs still outsourced would create demand for more Fluoristani goods and services—thus more jobs in Fluoristan, and better wages.

Once that happens, of course, most of the jobs outsourced to Fluoristan will be re-outsourced to someplace where they're still cheap, leaving Uncle Izblk not earning $25 instead of the $6 he used to not earn before all this started.

Watch this space for the Uncle Quznat column.

Floored by Flooring

ᴖᴖᴖ

In today's episode, Uncle Al experiences the thrill of victory (over his kitchen floor) and the agony of the feet.

Readers may be accustomed to reading of Uncle Al's culinary triumphs in the Taste section. Today's tale of splendor in the grease is set in the kitchen as well, but it has a somewhat different focus.

It begins several months ago when Uncle Al was whipping up a mixture of oil, vinegar and garlic in his blender. Something caught his attention, and he turned suddenly, knocking the blender over and spilling several cups of really oily vinaigrette onto his kitchen carpet.

The vinaigrette disappeared instantly into the carpet, and his attempts to blot it up with paper towels were fruitless (or maybe bootless, and certainly hootless, since Uncle Al wasn't laughing).

For several days, Uncle Al was able to ignore the matter of the vinaigrette-eating carpet. In fact, the kitchen actually smelled great. But he was quite sure that this aspect of the matter would not long remain so positive, and he sought the stain-removal advice of a colleague versed in such matters.

"Do you love this carpet?" she asked.

"Heck, no!" he replied. "I hate it. It came with the house. I just haven't gotten around to doing anything about it."

"Well, this is your chance," she said, "because the vinaigrette isn't going to go away."

Over the next several days, Uncle Al ripped, yanked, tore and scraped out the carpeting. The effort came none too soon; it was beginning to smell less like an Italian restaurant and more like the alley behind an Italian restaurant.

What was under the carpet, of course, was not what Uncle Al fervently hoped he would find—lovely hardwood flooring. It was linoleum. Really ugly linoleum. Covered with large patches of an intricate raised pattern of glue and pulled-off backing from the carpet.

Having been through a long and very painful linoleum-removal project once in his life, and there appearing to be nothing worth saving under the linoleum anyway, Uncle Al elected to go in the other direction and put new flooring *over* it. He removed the glue and carpet backing from the linoleum by dint of several days' occasional labor with laundry detergent (a solvent he discovered by accident—never mind—after more sensible ones failed to do much). The kitchen floor was now spotless (but still really ugly) and thus very ready to be covered.

As a next step, he purchased one of the ten boxes of the prefinished laminated flooring that the project would entail—both to commit himself to getting the horrible linoleum concealed and to get an advance peek at the detailed instructions packed inside.

He learned that the tongue-and-groove flooring had to be stapled down with a special staple gun that fit perfectly into the groove of each piece. What a neat idea! What a neat tool! What a surprise Uncle Al got when he priced it! It cost more than $200, and he'd probably never use it again. And it runs on compressed air, so he'd have to rent a compressor every time he wanted to use it (although he probably wouldn't again; see previous sentence).

After looking quite a while without success, during which (difficult as it might have been to imagine this earlier) the ugly linoleum seemed to get even uglier, he finally found a rental place that had the special staple gun.

That Friday night, before he was to pick up the gun, he moved everything but the stove and refrigerator out of the kitchen (the appliances would move around the kitchen as the work progressed), cleaned the linoleum again (boy, it was ugly!) and checked over his other preparatory work.

Readers who expect to find that Uncle Al forgot to cut a bit off the bottom of the door, to allow for the higher floor, will be sorely disappointed. Readers who expect to find that Uncle Al forgot to cut a notch out of the cabinets over the refrigerator, to allow it to fit back into that tight space when it was on top of the new flooring, will be delighted. Hey, one out of two; he decided to do the second thing later, while the refrigerator was out of the way.

He went to bed all a-tingle.

Saturday morning Uncle Al was off bright and early to rent the staple gun and the (incredibly heavy) compressor. He almost had to return, not very early and not at all bright, to have somebody show him how to put the staples in the staple gun, but there weren't all that many possibilities and it was only 35 years since he got his electrical engineering degree, so eventually he figured it out.

The flooring began to go into place, easily and rather well (after Uncle Al stopped jumping out of his skin whenever the compressor suddenly roared to life). But early progress was deceptive. Each piece was only 2¼ inches wide, and thus in a 10½-foot-wide floor, there were 57 courses of lumber to staple, each consisting of three or four random-length pieces, and almost every course involved sawing a few inches off a board at one end.

Uncle Al actually began stapling at about 10:30 a.m. He took short lunch and dinner breaks and a few others, and once in a while he stopped stapling to move the stove, the refrigerator or both.

Early in the afternoon he began to notice that both his getting down and his rising up, instead of being mere transitions between kneeling and standing, were becoming noticeable events in themselves. He became aware that there were muscles—or perhaps a lack of muscles—in the fronts of his thighs.

By early evening he was so stiff that when he took a break to buy a cold drink at a convenience store (the refrigerator door being against a wall at the moment), he was glad it was dark and nobody was outside to see him lurching across the street, appearing to be either inebriated or imitating Walter Brennan in cheap shoes.

When he knocked off a little after midnight, with the end of the job in sight and four hours available in the morning before the 10:30 a.m. deadline for the return of the stapler and compressor, Uncle Al was fairly pleased with himself over the flooring, and fairly alarmed with himself about his near-inability to shift between standing and kneeling.

To kneel, he had to hold on to something or, if there was nothing to hold on to, he had to first bend over from the waist until he could brace his hands on the floor and then lower himself, slowly and surprisingly painfully. Getting up was at least as bad.

And was he ever surprised when he tried to climb the stairs to go to bed!

Alarmingly, coming downstairs in the morning was even worse!

It seemed to Uncle Al that, to punish him for wanting a wooden floor in his kitchen while millions go hungry, God had decided to introduce him to his quadriceps.

Moving much more slowly than he had the previous day, Uncle Al finished all of the floor except the parts close to the wall that the stapler couldn't do; he struggled to get the compressor and stapler out to his truck and returned them to the rental shop.

Driving back home after an embarrassingly long and creaky display of getting into the driver's seat, Uncle Al, at 58, realized that he was being treated to a foretaste of how it will feel to be 98 (or maybe 78 or 68). He realized, too, that the money he saved by installing the flooring himself might now be spent instead on pain relief and physical therapy, or perhaps even on home-delivered meals and one of those motorized chairs that stands you up even if parts of you don't feel like standing.

Maybe, he thought, this will be the kick I need to begin to exercise. Maybe my legs wouldn't be tied in knots after a mere 16 hours of squatting and kneeling if I had been in better shape. Or, he thought, maybe in the future I'll just carefully avoid opportunities to spend 16 hours squatting and kneeling.

In any case, he thought, shifting into hole-in-the-roof mode, right now I'm much too stiff to start exercising; and when I'm not so stiff I won't need to exercise.

As soon as Uncle Al cuts a notch out of the cabinets so he can roll the refrigerator back into its place—and after he finishes work on all the moldings and miscellaneous pieces—he is actually looking forward to spilling some vinaigrette on his new prefinished wood floor so he can just wipe it right up.

If he can bend down by then.

A Waltz in Two Flats

丷丷

Once more, dear friends, we lift the curtain to reveal one of mankind's darker interludes—a sad tale of man, machines, and the elements:

I had a 7:30 a.m. breakfast appointment one recent Friday, so I propelled myself out of bed so early that both the dog, who had built himself a nice nest of quilt, and my wife, who didn't need to leave until much later, remained deep asleep.

Oh, well, dark and cold though it was, I dressed and stumbled out the door. It was going to be a very busy day, but at least I had the weekend free. A man's gotta do what a man's gotta do. And, as my younger son, Dave, observed when he was about four, "So do a woman," but that is neither here nor there.

What *was* there was a very flat—wheel-on-the-ground—left-front tire. I stumbled, half-awake, back into the house, to change out of the suit I had put on in order to look vaguely professional and thus impress the person I was to interview. I know from previous experience that I do not change a tire without getting half the world's dirt on my hands and my pants, and I have only one suit that fits (and it doesn't fit very well, but that's another story).

Only when I got back outside was I awake enough to remember that the spare tire was in a rack under the truck that had never been unscrewed in the four years I'd had it (nor in the preceding four, I would bet), and would thus be very nicely rusted in place, and no fun at all trying to remove while on my back in the snow.

This meant that I would need to drive the convertible. I don't drive it in the winter, mostly to keep it from rusting even further, but this year for the additional reason that late this summer the edges of the cooling-fan blades began to rub against their plastic shroud when the engine was cold, creating a very startling sound and probably causing wear on some deeply hidden bearing; I figured I would crawl under the car some nice warm day next spring and adjust the shroud; meanwhile, it was an extra reason not to drive the car until warm weather set in.

So anyway, I had to use the Olds (my wife needed *her* car to go to work), but since it was only January I hadn't yet garaged it and it was resting under six or seven inches of snow, plus, I discovered, a layer of ice on the windshield under all the snow. Well, that's what we pay for living in this best of all possible states, I muttered, as I brushed and scraped the ice and snow off the windshield and hood, getting much of it up my coat sleeves.

There was no longer time to go change back into my impress-the-public suit; I climbed in and started the Olds, hearing immediately the scraping of the engine fan on the shroud and moments later a piercing howl from the heater fan.

I'd forgotten about that one. It often screams like a banshee.

Anyway, I drove the Olds to the conference, accompanied by one scraping fan and one screaming fan, and with snow blowing off the roof and trunk, to the annoyance of many other drivers (judging by their expressions as they passed me). Nobody at the conference asked why I wasn't wearing a suit, but I felt compelled to explain the situation to everyone I met.

Then I drove to work downtown, where I did what I do for the rest of the day. I stayed late, trying to wrap up loose ends, and left around 8 p.m.

To discover that the Olds had . . . a flat.

Unlike the truck, the Olds's spare tire is perfectly accessible and it was full of air. And the jack was handy, too. But there was no wrench for removing the lug nuts. I remembered then that, to prepare for a summer trip, I had transferred the lug wrench to . . . the truck. I gave up for the day, called home, and asked my wife to come and get me. When I got home I went to bed.

Next morning, a Saturday, I got up bright and early and took my wife's car to the convenience store and bought several cans of Fix-A-Flat—goop that you spray into a flat tire in the usually forlorn hope that the tire might inflate and stay inflated long enough to get to a service station.

I went home and emptied one into the flat on the truck: It actually worked! Amazing! In fact, after driving it around for a bit (warming the tire, per instructions and, not incidentally, waiting for a decent hour to wake my wife so she could drive over to the service station too, where I would leave the truck to get the tire fixed so I wouldn't have to walk home, after which she could drive me to the Olds, whose tire I could then inflate or change, whereupon I could drive it to the service station too, and then ride home from there with her—got me?), it occurred to me that the tire was holding up fine, so I needn't bother her. I would just drive downtown and change the Olds tire.

No, I realized, then I'd be downtown with two cars. That would be dumb.

So I waited until she had breakfasted, skipped moving the truck, and drove downtown with her and another can of Fix-A-

Flat. No luck: The Olds tire deflated as quickly as it inflated. It had to be changed. And I had forgotten to bring along the lug wrench from the truck. We drove home, I got in the truck and drove back downtown.

The weather was cold but not too bad, so I hauled out the Olds's spare, assembled the jack, and looked for the lug wrench in the truck. It wasn't there. No point in wondering where it was; I drove off in the truck and, after two unsuccessful stops, bought another one.

Back at the Olds, I jacked it up, realized I hadn't loosened the wheel nuts, tried to lower it, and discovered that the jack would not come down. No amount of prodding, banging, cranking on it or whining at it would help. I was beginning to get really cold and feeling distinctly unhappy when I had a sudden thought: The truck has a jack, too. I could jack the car up further on the truck's jack, then remove the car's jack. Bingo.

In fairly short order, I raised the Olds, removed its jack, lowered it on the truck jack, loosened the wheel nuts, raised it again on the truck jack, removed the flat tire, installed the spare, and lowered the truck jack. Done; the Olds was more or less fixed and the truck was at least temporarily drivable. But both needed to get to a service station to have tires repaired, and I was alone downtown.

I was correct earlier; being downtown with two cars was dumb.

No, friends, I did not repeat my performance of last summer in which I leapfrogged the two vehicles home by driving one two blocks, walking back and getting the other one, driving it four blocks, walking back and getting the other one, driving it four blocks, etc. I have learned much since then.

I left the Olds where it was, drove home and went to bed.

I spent Sunday in motionless bliss. Monday morning I got a lift to work, and after work drove the Olds to the service station, where my wife met me and drove me home. A few more jockeying trips will get the Olds home and the truck to the service station and back, and then everything will be fine.

As I look around this pain-filled world, with bombing in Iraq, ethnic warfare in Bosnia, clan conflict, anarchy and starvation in Somalia, the Balkanization of much of the former Soviet bloc, and recession and unemployment here at home, I am able to take great comfort in one thing:

At least I can't afford three cars.

Looking for Closure

ⲧⲧⲧ

The other day Uncle Al was half-listening to TV, as is his habit, and only occasionally looking up from whatever he was reading—something like *Harry Potter and the Giant Pain in the Patoot,* or *DRAT: Warner Bros. Cartoons from the Viewpoint of the Coyote*—when these bits of an announcer's voice broke through:

"Dermabond may not be appropriate . . . certain sensitivities . . ."

The half or less of his brain that was listening apparently recognized the hallmark of a medical-products ad (one of Uncle Al's favorite kinds) and convinced the other half to pay attention, so he heard and remembered the rest long enough to jot it down:

"Ask the emergency-room doctor if Dermabond liquid stitches is right for you."

Good gracious, Uncle Al thought. (Actually, he thought something a bit stronger than that, but he doesn't want you to be offended.) It's bad enough, he went on thinking, that people go into doctors' offices asking if Synthamoxophil could be prescribed for any condition they have, because they saw a Synthamoxophil ad showing beautiful people bounding through meadows and they would like to bound through meadows and meet beautiful people.

And, Uncle Al thought further (when Uncle Al manages to start thinking, it's hard for him to stop), it's bad enough that men ask doctors how they can qualify for the product that warns on its TV ad to seek immediate medical help if what it does lasts more than four hours. (The ad on TV is quite specific, but as he has a family audience Uncle Al will not describe what the product is supposed to do for less than four hours. You're entirely welcome.)

Now, anyway, Uncle Al concluded to himself (if someone else had been there, Uncle Al might have said all this aloud, and he wouldn't be stuck with this endless interior monologue), on top of all of that, now people bleeding all over emergency rooms are being asked to engage hospital staffers in a lively discussion of the merits of various methods of wound closure!

Uncle Al imagines that fairly few people will see much benefit in starting this exchange of views, particularly because they'd have to do so while their wounds were still open, but he decided to look at the Web site of the product, which he learned is really 2-octyl cyanoacrylate, a more flexible and infection-inhibiting version of Super Glue.

Dermabond's manufacturer (Ethicon—a Johnson & Johnson company) takes the notion well past the remarkable, winding up deeply into the unbelievable. It provides, on the Dermabond Web site, scripts for asking about Dermabond in various situations (not just in the emergency room). Among them:

"Ask for Dermabond at any point during your emergency treatment. Ask the admitting nurse if they use Dermabond. 'I've heard of an innovative "skin glue" called Dermabond that can be used instead of stitches to close cuts. Do you use it at this hospital?'"

And,

"Following the cleansing and evaluation of your wound, your doctor will discuss the treatment process. This is also a good time to ask if Dermabond is an option. 'Doctor, I've heard of an innovative "skin glue" called Dermabond that can be used instead of stitches to close wounds. Can it be used to treat this wound?'"

(Uncle Al suspects that until now there have been very few uses of the word "innovative" by persons in the horizontal orientation on hospital gurneys.)

Several questions arise here:

Does Ethicon imagine people copying this banter onto little Miranda-warning wallet cards, on the chance that they will find themselves (a) having sustained gaping wounds, (b) in no particular hurry to have them closed, (c) not sure how to broach the subject of closure preferences with medical personnel, and (d) succeeding, in those conditions, at finding their wallets?

What should the patient do if the answer to a "Do you use it?" inquiry is "No"? Get up and leave, holding the wound shut with Vise-Grips? Mumble something about doctors not keeping up with the fine products of Johnson & Johnson? Ask the doctor whether he or she has any Super Glue?

What is the patient supposed to do if the answer to a "Do you use it?" inquiry is a little more unpleasant? For example: "I'll tell you what, pal: I won't tell you how to write peculiar newspaper columns [or your job description here]; don't tell me how to close a wound."

Is there a face-saving remark somewhere on Dermabond's Web site that keeps that situation from getting really ugly? And is there a comeback there for the inevitable "And what medical school did you graduate from?"

Apparently there isn't, and that's a real shame, as Uncle Al would have found it useful even in circumstances unrelated to gaping wounds. Pointing out that "And what medical school did you graduate from?" ends in a preposition just doesn't have the stinging quality that Uncle Al feels is required in this situation. And it might be a bit too low to note that although you lack a medical degree, no one has died while in your care.

If it turns out that Dermabond's approach somehow succeeds in getting the product used by doctors who hadn't considered it before, Uncle Al is, unfortunately, able to imagine similar TV appeals and Web site scripts turning up on behalf of other products.

For example: "Ask the dessert chef if he or she uses Little Debbie products. 'I've heard of an innovative snack cake called Little Debbie Double Chocolate Swiss Cake Rolls. Do you prepare desserts using Little Debbie Double Chocolate Swiss Cake Rolls?'"

Be sure not to ask this while the chef is slicing something. Or, if you do, have your Dermabond wallet card ready for when the ambulance arrives.

Striking a Lucky Bargain

I have detailed, on several previous occasions, the apparent disintegration of significant portions of my mental capacity. (At least I think I have; I don't really remember.)

Much of that deterioration is evidenced in my dealing with the dog I share with the woman who eventually became my second ex-wife. Lots of people talk to and for their dogs, but I seem to have gone quite a bit farther down that one-way street in recent days.

I must explain that, like many dogs, Lucky, who is a sheltie-golden retriever mixture—sort of a short golden retriever—greatly relishes his twice-a-day walks, often tugging rather hard in another direction when I try to turn us toward home. On one such occasion recently I whined, "Oh, come on, Lucky, enough's enough."

"Look, Al," he explained patiently, "sniffing trees is my only hobby. I don't have opposable thumbs, so it's not as if I could take up model trains."

"Good point, Lucky," I acknowledged.

"Thanks a bunch, Al," he replied, his voice dripping with sarcasm.

I need also to explain that Lucky recently had a small growth removed on his neck, so he's missing a patch of fur and there are a few stitches in the middle of the bare spot. They're coming out soon, and he's fine, but meanwhile I don't want to irritate the wound, so I've loosened his collar a lot.

The other morning when we came to the heading-for-home corner, I turned and Lucky didn't. In fact, he dug in his feet, muttering, "I'm not done yet," and the loosened collar threatened to pull forward over his ears and come right off. So I relented.

That's when I heard myself forming a sentence that troubles me quite a bit in terms of my mental state:

"Oh, OK, Lucky," I said grudgingly, turning back to let him go sniffing trees down an extra block, "but you owe me."

I note with some relief that only a few seconds passed before I realized that the concept of a dog paying back a favor might be a stretch. But then I burst out laughing, and I'm not sure that laughing out loud at an exchange between me and the dog is any better than having the exchange in the first place.

When I thought about it later, it reminded me of a joke I heard a few months ago that led to an interesting interchange with my son Dave.

I hope nobody will be offended because the joke involves a prostitute. Nobody gets victimized, demeaned, or otherwise lessened in the course of this bit of fictional humor, and nobody is held up as an unrealistic example of anything bad. But I can't change the joke to remove the prostitute, because the whole point of this story is how to change the joke to remove the prostitute.

Suspended judgments in place, panel? Thanks. Here goes:

A guy is in a seedy hotel in Las Vegas and sees, leaning against the wall next to the elevator, a beautiful woman who makes it clear by appearance, word and deed that she is a call girl. She gives him a very meaningful look; he asks her what she charges, and she says, "A thousand dollars."

"A thousand dollars!" he says, shocked. "Boy, that's a lot of money. But . . . how about five hundred dollars?"

She thinks it over. "Well," she says, finally, "OK, but I'm not going to make anything on it."

I liked the joke, and so did Dave and one or two of my friends, but most people just didn't seem to recognize "I'm not going to make anything on it" as a punch line. Some folks even said, "And . . . ?"

Dave is trained as an actor and, like me, is perhaps inordinately interested in what makes something funny, so we spent a little time talking about it.

Based on a few remarks from people who didn't get the joke, we speculated that what went wrong was that they didn't see that the woman's job didn't involve significant expenses. That's why it was funny when she claimed she wouldn't make any money if she cut her price.

"But she has to rent a room," these people would argue. "She has to buy cheesy outfits so she can lean against elevator walls in them."

Dave and I agreed that, to fix the joke, we needed to substitute for the prostitute someone who more clearly has no expenses.

One of us suggested a Three-Card Monte dealer. Nobody could imagine that a person encounters lots of expenses suckering people into guessing which of three cards is which.

Although that was better, I saw a flaw in it: "There are probably lots of people who don't know what Three-Card Monte is," I said. "In fact, I bet your mother doesn't know what it is."

"I bet you ten bucks she does," he said.

"I don't want to bet ten bucks on that," I said. "How about a dollar?"

"Well, OK," Dave said, a smile of complete victory appearing on his face, "but I'm not going to make anything on it."

The Struggle to Embrace Change

Time to check in again on the declining mental state of one of my favorite personalities: me.

To fully comprehend the depths to which I have now sunk, we must go back in time a few weeks to a day when I was visiting a friend in the hospital and found myself ravenously hungry. Neither the cafeteria nor the coffee shop was open, but there was a vending machine room and a fully stocked candy machine. Great.

Unfortunately, I determined, I had only 20 cents in change. But there was a dollar-bill changer. Saved again. Unfortunately, I determined, I had only a $5 bill. But the machine accepted fives. Saved one more time. I fed it my five and out came a huge pile of coins, most of which I dumped into my left front pocket. I bought a candy bar, felt extremely lucky, and went about my business.

The next day, while walking across a parking lot, I heard a coin hit the pavement, then another. Before I could bend down to retrieve the first one, they were all cascading down my leg. Apparently the pocket had had only limited scrutiny from Inspector No. 12, and that had been quite a while ago. What was left of the pocket simply couldn't hold up to the strain of $4.60 in change.

I chased down most of the money (what looked like a dime came to rest in a grease puddle under a truck, and I abandoned it). I wish I could tell you that I did not dump the whole handful right back into the faulty pocket; in fact, I did manage to catch myself with most of the money still in my fist, and I put all of that—and the coins I re-retrieved from the pavement—into my right-hand jacket pocket.

Time, as it tends to do, moved on. One day not long ago I was setting out in the morning and reached into my jacket pocket for my car keys. They weren't there.

There was my ungainly set of keys to many, many things (most of which I could not identify if my life depended on it, some of which I probably no longer own, and some of which may have long since been destroyed). And there was that still large lump of change. (Because I seldom have my jacket on when I need change—my major such expense being candy bars at work—the bucketful of money had remained more or less intact in my jacket pocket.) But my slim separate set of car keys was not there. All those coins made it difficult to be certain, so I fished through the pocket twice more.

Nope, no car keys.

I shifted the stuff in my left hand to my right hand and went through my left-hand jacket pocket. An interesting collection of candy wrappers, plastic bags for dog walking, used twist ties (I'm starting a collection), and similar detritus. No car keys.

I shifted the stuff in my right hand back to my left hand and went through my right front pants pocket. Lucky acorn, handkerchief, money clip with "John Cowles" engraved on it (purchased for me for $3 at a garage sale by the woman who was to become my second ex-wife). No car keys.

Stuff from left hand back to right hand. Left front pants pocket. Nothing—only hole in pocket. Oh, *those* pants. Gotta get that fixed. Uh-oh! Could the keys have fallen through that hole? Yipe! And I hadn't gotten around to making duplicate keys since I discovered (several years ago) that I had only one set.

Now in desperation, shift hands, back to the right-hand jacket pocket. This time take all the keys out; no car keys stuck to them. Take all the coins out; no car keys stuck to them, either.

Shift hands again, getting ready to recheck the left-hand jacket pocket, meanwhile in a growing panic (How will I get to work? How will I get new keys made? What is to become of me?), when I realize that what I have been shifting from hand to hand through all of this is . . . the #$*@ car keys.

I am resting comfortably now, watching *Rockford Files* reruns on television and hoping to return soon to a productive life. As soon as I find my checkbook.

Martian to a Different Drummer

ㅜㅜㅜ

Much scientific speculation was scientifically speculated some time ago over the announcement that microscopic structures found in a meteorite recovered in Antarctica might be elementary forms of life from Mars.

Nothing I have seen bothers to give us a clue as to what makes scientists think that the rock, which is said to look like a potato, came from Mars, as opposed to Pluto or one of the Pleasure Planets of Deneb, or, for that matter, North Dakota.

Now, before you discount the possibility that a meteorite that looks like a potato came to Antarctica from North Dakota, as opposed to from Mars, consider how very many potatoes come from North Dakota, as opposed to Mars, and how much closer North Dakota is to Antarctica.

Then consider the very unlikely explanation that has been offered of how a piece of Mars supposedly wound up in Antarctica (this is different from what makes anyone think it came from Mars in the first place; this is how it could have got to Antarctica from there):

According to a diagram published in the newspaper, the potato-shaped rock "was dislodged from Mars 16 million years ago by a comet or asteroid and escaped Martian gravity. It probably circled the sun for a long time before its orbit changed under the gravitational pull of other planets, so that it finally crashed into Earth."

Well!

If I told you that a potato found on Mars got there because a comet or asteroid dislodged it from North Dakota with so much force that it escaped Earth's gravity, you'd have a hard time recalling the last time something like that happened, right? You would also find it fairly difficult to believe that despite all of the empty space out there in empty space (take a look up some night), it managed—even "a long time" later—to wind up on Mars.

But let's go ahead and admit the possibility that the Antarctica rock really is a piece of Mars. After all, in a universe in which nature or chance or God has produced both Albert Schweitzer and Madonna, clearly anything is possible.

Let's move on to something more interesting. I heard a scientist on National Public Radio offer the possibility that if the Martian rock really does contain primitive life-forms, then perhaps terrestrial life originated on Mars—and, in fact, perhaps life on Earth developed only after the planet was "seeded" with Martian life.

If that's possible, though, it's also possible that at the time Earth was "seeded" with Martian life, native Earth life was already in existence. (Why not?)

That would mean that there could exist simultaneously life-forms truly indigenous to Earth and others that are ultimately of Martian ancestry. And millions of generations and interbreedings later, they might still be subtly (but distinctly) different.

The fearless Al Sicherman column herewith offers guidelines for telling whether your boss is a Martian. (Apologies to Jeff Foxworthy and the *Weekly World News*.)

- If your boss says, "It's not the humidity, it's the heat," your boss could be a Martian.
- If your boss's music collection consists entirely of eight-track tapes featuring the work of Slim Whitman, chances are your boss is a Martian.
- If your boss lives at the lake all year and moves to an apartment in the city for three weeks in the summer, it's a good bet your boss is a Martian.
- If your boss remarks periodically that Attila did a lot of good things, he just went too far, you can be pretty sure your boss is a Martian.
- If your boss eats the watermelon seeds and spits out the juice, it's extremely likely that your boss is a Martian.
- If your boss puts on his or her pants both legs at a time, it's dollars to doughnuts that your boss is a Martian.
- If your boss separates the halves of an Oreo and eats the cookies first, somehow leaving the filling to eat last, your boss has just got to be a Martian.
- And if your boss gets a kind of faraway look whenever you mention potatoes or Antarctica, there's no doubt about it: Your boss is a Martian.

Getting Older in Multiple Ways

Upon opening a magazine recently, Uncle Al was confronted with an ad for an astonishing product: Nivea Visage Multiple Results All in One Anti-Aging Treatment.

Until that moment, all Uncle Al knew about Nivea was what he remembered from long ago, when, if you asked somebody in a drugstore if they had Nivea, they pointed to a stack of dark-blue jars next to the stack of dark-blue jars of Noxzema.

In puzzlement, Uncle Al dove into the haystack of un-digested, unverified and seldom-updated information we call the Internet and several hours later emerged clutching this nee-dle: It seems there are now more kinds of Nivea than there are flavors of Ragu red pasta sauce. Uncle Al is not kidding. Ragu appears to have 37 red pasta sauces. There seem to be 40 kinds of Nivea.

Yes. 40.

And Uncle Al is not counting multiple sizes. Plain old Nivea cream, in several sizes, is just one of the 40 Niveas.

(There need be no shame that we enjoy this astounding bounty of Nivea products while elsewhere people starve: It doesn't appear that any of the kinds of Nivea is edible.)

Before further discussing Nivea Visage Multiple Results All in One Anti-Aging Treatment, Uncle Al wanted to use the searingly brilliant searchlight of the deeply insightful Uncle Al column to illuminate all 39 other kinds of Nivea, but that turned out to take up more than half of the space that the searingly brilliant searchlight of the deeply insightful Uncle Al column gets to illuminate. So here's just a sample:

There are five varieties of Nivea Body Essential Care. They are: Sheer Moisture Lotion, for normal to dry skin; Original Lotion, for dry skin; Creamy Conditioning Oil, for very dry, flaky skin; Extra Enriched Lotion, for very dry, rough skin, and Original Skin Oil, for *severely* dry, chapped skin. Uncle Al isn't kidding. (He expects Nivea's next product introduction to be Creamy Light Crude Oil, for *scarily* dry, industrial-abrasive-grade skin.)

But it is Nivea Visage Multiple Results All in One Anti-Aging Treatment, one of five kinds of Nivea Visage Advanced Repair Care, that Uncle Al feels the need to discuss in some detail, in part because that's what was in the ad that started this whole mess.

Uncle Al must acknowledge that if anybody ought to be looking for Advanced Repair Care products, it's him. Even the most basic of the many repairs Uncle Al probably needs would surely cost much more than his deductible. But the other four Advanced Repair products seem to concentrate on wrinkles, and that isn't high on his agenda.

So if Multiple Results had not been the Advanced Repair product of which he first became aware, he probably would have gravitated to it anyway. What had made him sit up and take notice in the first place was the ad's headline: "Counter the multiple signs of aging all at once with the skin's own creatine."

The picture showed the bottle clearly labeled "All in One Anti-Aging Treatment." Uncle Al doesn't know (or care) any more about creatine than he does about, say, Lindsay Lohan, but a multiple-result anti-aging treatment sounded like a breath-taking medical breakthrough.

At a minimum, he would expect it to counter these signs of aging:

- Loss of hair (on head)
- Extra hair (in ears)
- Making groaning noise when standing up from comfy chair
- Falling asleep during weather forecast and then being wide awake at 4:30 a.m.
- Complaining about falling asleep during weather forecast and then being wide awake at 4:30 a.m.
- Inability to remember other signs of aging

Uncle Al rushed out and bought a small container (1.7 ounces) of Multiple Results, for an astounding $18.99 plus tax. That's $179 a pound! Still, for multiple anti-aging results, it might be money well spent.

He was annoyed to find that the instructions called for first using the Nivea SkinBalance Cleanser selected for his type of skin (there seem to be four, and maybe others in the Nivea for Men line, but Uncle Al isn't quite sure; at this point he was beginning to lose it), followed by Nivea Moisturizing Toner to clarify and refresh his skin, and only then was he to smooth Nivea Visage Multiple Results over his face and neck. All of this twice a day.

He really couldn't see spending another $12 acquiring extra products in order to use something called "all in one." So before applying Multiple Results he has washed his face with soap, then moisturized with water (it's 100 percent moisture;

can't do better than that—although he must acknowledge that after that he feels refreshed but not clarified). And every other day or so he has shaved, too.

After one day he had noticed three results (which he acknowledges is "multiple," but just barely):

- When he first applies Nivea Visage Multiple Results, his face stings a little. (To be fair, Nivea doesn't say all of the multiple results are positive.)
- He smells vaguely like a cosmetics department.
- Most noticeably, he has a thin layer of gunk on his face. Whenever he wipes his forehead (which he does, for example, after wrestling with a particularly nasty subordinate clause), his hand comes away with part of a visage's worth of Nivea.

But on Day 3 he noticed another result, making the results clearly multiple:

- He remembered another possible sign of aging: being easily persuaded to make questionable purchases.

Funnel Vision

Some months it doesn't pay to get out of bed.

I present for your edification and amusement the strange tale of the disappearing funnel. I tell it now for two compelling reasons: (1) It establishes an additional significant data point on the downward-racing graph of my mental acuity; (2) if I don't write this down, I won't remember it a week from now, when something like it is bound to happen again.

The scene: For reasons that are better left unexplained (trust me; you don't really want to know more than I'm going to tell you), there are three slow cookers full of vegetable oil on my basement floor. There is also a very large, empty plastic bottle into which that oil could go. In fact, it is the very bottle in which that oil was purchased.

My basement is such, at least right now, that three slow cookers full of vegetable oil do not really bring down its overall tone, if you get my drift. So the need to pour the oil back into the bottle is not based on neatness. Still, I'd like not to have hanging over me the prospect that one dark night I will trip over one (or, with my luck, two or three) of the slow cookers and spill several quarts of vegetable oil all over the basement's very tacky indoor-outdoor carpeting.

The slow cookers are on my basement floor because I decided one day that I was less likely to trip over them there than if they continued to sit, full of vegetable oil, on my kitchen floor, whose indoor-outdoor carpeting isn't quite as tacky as that in the basement.

The reason they needed to sit, full of vegetable oil, on either floor was that I couldn't find the funnel necessary for the tricky job of pouring the oil back into the plastic bottle.

I started looking for the funnel as soon as I had finished my task with the slow cookers. (Again I insist that you and I will both be better off if I don't explain what that task was.) I know that I have a funnel because not six months ago I had to buy one to put some previous vegetable oil back into its bottle. I was sure, at that time, that I already owned a funnel, but I couldn't find it, so I had to buy one.

So now—because I was not about to buy yet another funnel simply because I couldn't find the previous funnel, which replaced another funnel I couldn't find—every day for at least two weeks I went down into the basement and looked for the $#%@& funnel in even the most wildly unlikely places. Behind the furnace? No. In the closet full of miscellaneous cans of paint left behind by some previous home colorist? No. On any of the many shelves full of seldom-used kitchen tools? No, no, no. (I checked those especially often.)

Finally, after completely running out of hope, I decided to buy another #@%#@ funnel. Every time I went grocery shopping I scanned the shelves of kitchen gadgets looking for a funnel. No luck, at any of the stores I frequent—although I must admit that my enthusiasm for the task was so low that I didn't even ask anyone where the funnel department was.

Meanwhile, I felt sure that the likelihood of a multiquart oil spill was increasing with each additional day on which I lacked a funnel. Eventually, I knew, I would stumble over one or more of the slow cookers because I would forget that they were there.

So last weekend I bit the bullet and added to my errand list a quick trip to a discount store for a plastic funnel.

Of course, the store didn't stock plastic funnels sold singly. I was able to purchase only a set of three nested plastic funnels: A papa funnel, a mama funnel and an itty-bitty baby funnel, so teeny that I cannot imagine a use for it. Since I was in the store, of course, I also purchased $28 worth of miscellaneous stuff I didn't know I needed and that I never would have bought if I hadn't gone to the store for the funnel.

When I got home, I hurried down to the basement with my new set of funnels. Finally confronted with the task I had been thinking about for so long, however, I decided to have lunch (and maybe dinner) before I really did it.

So I put the funnels down on a shelf, next to . . . a funnel.

There it sat—two inches from where I put my hand. I don't know whether it was the funnel I couldn't find six months ago or the funnel I bought six months ago to replace the funnel I couldn't find, and which I subsequently couldn't find, either, if you follow me.

Now I have five funnels, one of which is lost. But if a few months from now you see me wandering vaguely about, appearing to look for something, ask me whether it's a funnel.

And if it is, be kind.

Buns Not Found in the Oven

᠕᠕᠕

I knew there was something going on last year, when an issue of *Glamour* magazine had this headline on its cover: "A Better Butt Fast." At the time I merely mused that I hadn't previously associated the words "butt" and "glamour."

But now (or butt now) I can see that I had only seen what was on the surface—I hadn't gotten to the backside of the news. Meanwhile, I had also merely noted in passing the existence of a workout videotape called *Buns of Steel*. My only reaction to that, I think, was that the possibility of my attaining steel buns seemed about as low as did the desirability of doing so.

I can see now how wrong I was. What opened my eyes was a chance visit to the videotape rack at a discount store. I simply had no idea:

There is an entire *Buns of Steel* industry.

It's true; I am not joking. At this store I could select from the following *Buns of Steel* tapes (as distinct from the somewhat less intimidating *Legs of Steel* tapes, the baffling *Abs of Steel* tapes, the half-baffling *Arms and Abs of Steel* tapes, and the absolutely frightening *Thighs of Steel* tape):

• *Buns of Steel, Original*/ Intense target toning with less aerobics.

(How the original can have "less" is a mystery that only our nation's wisest bundits might be able to solve.)

• *Buns of Steel 2*/ Beginners' step workout: intense target toning with low-impact aerobics.

(I don't know what "target toning" is. In fact, I don't know what either "target" or "toning" is. I'm pretty sure I know what a beginner is.)

• *Buns of Steel 3* / Buns and more: concentrated workout for abs, buns, and thighs.

(What on earth is an ab? Do I have one? How many do I have? Do girls have abs? Are they nicer than boys' abs?)

• *Buns of Steel 4* / Advanced: super advanced workout for super definition and muscle tone.

(Butt seriously: Just how well does anybody's butt need to be defined? "That's a butt, right over there" generally does the trick. Or, to paraphrase the words of Associate Justice Potter Stewart, in an opinion for the U.S. Supreme Court, I may not be able to define a butt, but I know one when I see it.)

• *Buns of Steel 5* / Beginners / Beginners' workout: safe, easy, effective.

(Here's where I began to get really scared. It hadn't occurred to me that any of these tapes might not be safe. So *Buns of Steel 5* is safe. What about all the others? If I bought *Buns of Steel 3,* am I in some kind of danger? Will my buns fall off? What about my abs? And if my abs fell off, would I notice?)

• *Buns of Steel 6* / Intermediate / Step workout: fat-burning and conditioning.

(I'm not at all sure I want my fat burned. That sounds distinctly unpleasant. Wafted away would be more my choice. Caused to disappear with no effort, no ill effect and no regret is perhaps a bit too specific, but certainly more what I have in mind in the fat-loss department.)

• *Buns of Steel 7* / Intermediate-Advanced / Step workout: low-impact aerobics, lower body toning.

(I know how you would know that you were a beginner in

the *Buns of Steel* business, which means you ought to concentrate on *Buns of Steel 2* or *5*, and I suppose you can tell when you have advanced buns, and thus need *Buns of Steel 4*, and probably you can tell if you're between those points and have intermediate buns, which would point you to *Buns of Steel 6*. But do we really have in this great nation a large number of people who see themselves as having intermediate-advanced buns?)

So what's the bottom line?

That ought to be clear enough: If people are willing to spend time and money on their buns (I presume that most people buy these tapes for themselves—not as a hint to others about *their* buns), they ought to be willing to spend similar amounts of money on their other body parts.

Watch your discount store for these tapes from Uncle Al: *Appendix of Steel, Cast-Iron Stomach* and *Head Like a Concrete Block.*

It's All Dog Food

ᴄᴄᴄ

Just before Christmas I recommended to readers of the Taste section that if they had oodles of time and were to be guests at someone else's holiday table, they might want to prepare a Bûche de Noël, the knock-your-socks-off French version of the Yule log cake roll.

It represents a big chunk of a day of increasingly fussy work in the kitchen, but it sure makes folks go "Ooooh!"

To my great pleasure I heard later from a number of people who had made the cake and were delighted. Then I opened what proved to be a three-page handwritten letter.

"Uh-oh," I thought, "here comes trouble." Long letters usually are unpleasant: Happy people just say "Thanks"; angry people go into detail.

It turned out not to be an angry letter but a tale, to wit:

The writer had spent most of the day before Christmas making the Bûche de Noël. She packed it up Christmas morning, along with presents and cranberries, for the drive to her kids' farm, where her granddaughter was going to help her with the final stages of cake decorating.

She let her dog out of the car, gave the large resident dog a hug, and carried bags of toys into the house for five minutes of "Merry Christmas, Grandma." When she returned to the car, the door of which she had failed to nudge fully shut, she found that the family dog had removed the box containing the food and was happily eating the Bûche de Noël.

Her daughter just laughed, she said, because, at Thanksgiving, Grandma's dog had gotten a couple of bites out of the turkey.

Clearly, all the people involved in that story are dog lovers—careless dog lovers, perhaps, and they'll surely be more watchful in the future, for the dogs' sakes as well as to protect the food—but these are people willing to forgive a dog for following what surely seemed to the dog to be a fine idea.

It is a group in which I include myself.

Lucky, a well-bred—actually crossbred but well-mannered—medium-size dog, now rooms at my house when the woman who usually buys his dinner (my latest ex-wife) goes out of town. Sometimes all three of us still dine together.

Other than becoming rather barkish in his senior years, Lucky is a very fastidious individual, who will not take food off a coffee table—even though it is just about the right height to allow him to ease his nose onto it, and even if there's nobody else in the room.

Once, many years ago, when he was new on the job, Lucky fished in the garbage bag for a steak bone. When an adult entered the kitchen, there he was with what he'd managed to latch on to—a corncob. He was humiliated, and nothing like that has ever happened again. He doesn't touch the garbage, even when nobody's home.

Neither of his current parents can take any credit for his training; he was two years old when he came from the Humane Society, exactly like a bargain computer, with software preloaded and no manuals. He had rules; we just had no idea what they were.

He was perfectly well behaved at first. But after a few weeks, when it became clear that he was housebroken and didn't paw or chew at things, he was invited to join people on the couch. Apparently he came with a rule against that. As soon as we urged him to break that rule, he began to do all the other things he'd been trained never to do—at least not in the house.

Somehow that got straightened out, and a few shots of carpet cleaner took care of the evidence.

As for eating, he regards as his own anything that is handed to him or is on the floor, and he absolutely believes that nothing else belongs to him. We never even warn him about not eating food from places he can reach; he just doesn't do it.

That has worked fine until one day a few weeks ago. His two people were sharing a plateful of spaghetti for supper, but it proved to be way too much for us, and the leftovers were headed back to the kitchen from the coffee table. His mother got up with the spaghetti, realized that she forgot a glass on the coffee table, and started (for no good reason) to set the plate down on the floor to turn around and get the glass.

The plate no sooner brushed the carpet than Lucky zoomed in, more or less out of nowhere, grabbed the entire mound of spaghetti and began trying frantically to gulp it down. Not only was it bigger than anything he'd ever eaten, it was spaghetti; no matter how much he gulped at it, it just kept on coming.

Most canine facial expressions are open to a wide range of interpretation. Do ears up and head cocked, for example, indicate alertness, puzzlement, or an attempt to sucker you into providing a treat?

But there was no way to read Lucky struggling with the overwhelming load of spaghetti other than "Holy Moley!"

His mother was momentarily convulsed by the spectacle,

so a few seconds—and most of the spaghetti—went by before she pulled herself together and yanked the plate away, trailing spaghetti from both plate and dog.

I felt sorry for him: He wasn't breaking any rules—his or ours—and not only didn't he get to finish the food, it practically choked him. I wanted to tell him not to feel bad—that spaghetti is hard to eat without a fork.

In fact, for his sake I kind of wish it had been a Bûche de Noël. Or at least Spaghetti-Os.

Aspiring to Be a Big Loser

ᴖᴖᴖ

I stand in awe of recent developments in the world of finance:

- Nicholas Leeson, a 28-year-old trader in Singapore, lost $1 billion and caused the collapse of a centuries-old British bank by trading in derivatives based on the Japanese stock and interest-rate markets.
- Robert Citron, the treasurer of Orange County, California, cost the county $2 billion by investing in derivatives based on mortgage-backed securities.
- Some guy (whose name I have misplaced) at Procter & Gamble, maker of Crest, Tide and Pampers, lost a relatively paltry $102 million when derivatives based on U.S. treasury notes and German interest rates went south.

Anybody whose job is important enough that he could lose billions—or, really, even just hundreds of millions—of dollars deserves a little respect.

In my present position, I am forced to acknowledge, about the only thing of value that I lose is ballpoint pens.

I probably lose one every week, which seems pretty frequent, but the dollar amount is not at all impressive: Assuming that each of the pens in question had another week's ink left when I lost it after a week, and that each cost $1 (so that each loss wasted 50 cents), the 48 pens mislaid each year (I get vacation, during which I abstain from losing company pens) would bring the newspaper's loss to $24 a year.

Pretty pitiful. Can I do better?

If I lost an almost-full pen at the end of every day, each would represent a loss of 90 cents, times 240 (48 five-day weeks), or $216. Not much more impressive.

How about a pen every minute? Call each one worth the full $1 (let's not quibble over a minute's worth of ink); 48 weeks of five eight-hour days amount to $115,200 in lost pens. Now we're getting somewhere.

If I could lose a pen every second (I know I could manage that if I put my mind to it—say by just throwing them around the room), that would come to $6,912,000 a year. That's still not in the Leeson-Citron league, but along with the fact that I wouldn't have time to do anything but lose pens, it'd be enough to make my boss notice. It would, however, require quite a bit of space to throw pens into (or maybe an open window to throw them out of), as well as a staff of folks dedicated to getting me a new box of pens every 10 or 12 seconds.

I guess I have to face facts: Losing pens just doesn't have enough financial clout. I need to do some real financial speculation to lose enough money to earn some serious attention.

I don't think the fact that I'm in the newspaper column business should preclude me from losing large amounts of company money in pork-belly futures and interest-rate swaps. If betting on the deutschmark makes more sense to a manufacturer of toothpaste, soap and disposable diapers than trying to sell more toothpaste, soap and disposable diapers, it ought to be good enough for me and the *Star Tribune*.

OK, what'll it be? Let's be clear here: Just buying stocks or bonds isn't speculative enough to bring down a really nice, juicy, gigantic house of cards. There are actual investments involved there.

I need something much nastier than that if I want to lose really big. Something that involves pure speculative risk-taking with no hint of any underlying worth or meaningful contribution to the economy. Just winning and losing.

Something like agreeing to sell a billion tons of pork bellies (which I don't have) and hoping that I can first buy them cheaper than what I agreed to sell them for.

If that happens I make a lot of money for the *Star Tribune,* and they give me a coffee mug.

If instead the pork bellies cost more than I agreed to sell them for, that's my big break: I lose a couple trillion dollars, but my name and picture appear on network TV, I fend off ambush interviews with *Inside Edition* and *A Current Affair,* and I am mentioned in newspapers all over the country—except the *Star Tribune,* which will have folded.

I'll have to be prepared to start over somewhere else in case that happens, but my needs are modest. All I'll require is a packed suitcase, forged identity papers, plane tickets for somewhere in South America—and a large supply of ball-point pens.

Top Down in the 8-Track Lane

⌐⌐⌐

After numerous adventures with my rusting 1971 Oldsmobile Cutlass convertible, I sold it recently to someone more likely to catch up with the rust and other things that I had tried, unsuccessfully, to ignore.

I was reluctant to part with it; we had been through a lot together. But as it aged, it developed a penchant for stranding me in strange places, and because I was aging along with it, I became somewhat less tolerant of that proclivity. And, in addition to its occasional mechanical problems, it got lousy gas mileage. And it was pretty darn big.

But in the summer, with the top down, as nature intended, it was a swell car.

So when I decided I had to sell it, I was bereft. I immediately turned around and bought another old convertible, this one a 1975 full-size Chevrolet. It is absolutely humongous. I used to say that the Olds was sort of a boat. The Chevy is the boat that the Olds was sort of. When I park it, I feel as if I ought to throw out mooring lines. I don't even want to calculate what kind of mileage I'm getting.

But it's gorgeous, and in the summer, with the top down, as nature intended, it's a swell car.

Among its snazzy features is a factory-installed AM/FM/ 8-track tape player. It wasn't working when I got it, and there were no tapes, but I got it going and I've been buying tapes at garage sales and antique shops. I now have a small collection.

I'm not sure exactly when the 8-track began to fade beneath the consumer horizon, but I'm hoping to amass a collection of tapes from 1975 or before. I must confess—or proclaim—that I pretty much stopped following popular music when I left my college dorm in 1963. Much music has been made since then without my specific awareness. I look upon this 8-track project as my chance to bring my musical taste up to 1975.

I can report that the Captain and Tennille look to have some staying power, and that Sonny and Cher are another promising musical couple.

To inaugurate the car, and to show it to my son Dave, I drove it out to New York for a short vacation. We took a weekend trip to Montreal and back, and had a high old time eating convenience-store snacks and playing the 8-track.

To my great relief we did not encounter the suspicious Canadian border security we met when we drove to Winnipeg from Minneapolis seven years ago in the Olds. (I had picked Dave up in Milwaukee, where he was living with his mother.) That exchange went something like this:

"Where are you from?"

"Minneapolis," I said.

"Both from Minneapolis?"

"No," Dave said, "I'm from Milwaukee."

"OK, where were you born?"

"Milwaukee," I said.

"Both born in Milwaukee?"

"No," Dave said, "I was born in Minneapolis."

"You wanna pull in over there?"

The guard had me open the car's trunk. Rummaging through my suitcase, asking small questions as he went—How long will you be staying in Canada? Are you bringing in any alcohol?—he came across several notebooks. He held them up, his expression asking for an explanation.

"I'm a writer," I said.

He paged slowly through each one. All were blank.

"No thoughts?" he asked with heavy sarcasm, sounding as if he had just nailed an atom spy. I half-expected a slap across the face and a "Perhaps *this* will refresh your memory!"

Instead, a moment later, he sighed and wished us a nice vacation.

But on the current trip, returning from Montreal to New York, after the border guard asked a few desultory "What is the purpose of your trip?" questions, she popped one apparently designed to catch Canadians trying to sneak south in American cars:

"What is your license plate number?"

"I really don't know," I said. "I just bought the car."

I got a look that said, "You just bought a 1975 car?"

It would have made a more symmetrical story if she had then said "You wanna pull in over there?" but honesty compels me to report that she waved us through. I think I probably look like the kind of guy whose car is 21 years old. At least.

Anyway, after getting back to New York, and two late Sunday night back-and-forth trips across the George Washington Bridge hauling a free trundle bed from the apartment of a friend of Dave's in Washington Heights to his own flat in Jersey City (a convertible with the top down is a great, if rather public, cargo vehicle), I set off again for Minneapolis, where I soon had the car in the garage for the winter.

It was a good trip, the car ran OK, and it was really good to travel a couple of days with Dave, eating junk food and telling each other stories. Now that he's out of college and starting a career, I suppose there won't be tons more such trips. Sigh.

In the course of the trip I made two discoveries. One is that the Land of Make-Believe is real, and is about 20 miles east of Saranac Lake in upstate New York. (I don't know what the heck it is either, but it's on highway signs and road maps.)

The other discovery, due to the 8-track player, is that songs I have heard on commercials had more lyrics than I was aware of. There is more to Carly Simon's "Anticipation," for example, than the part that is played behind the Heinz ketchup not coming out of the bottle. It includes the line "These are the good old days."

I guess maybe they were.

How to Sink a Vacation

ʿʿʿ

Uncle Al has had recent occasion to reexamine what he has previously thought of as one of nature's basic rules (alongside the Law of Gravity, Archimedes' Principle and No Shirt, No Shoes, No Service).

He has hitherto firmly believed that every home-repair or home-improvement project that involves both a new purchase and an existing installation (replacing a light fixture, for example) requires three trips to the hardware store.

What he has recently come to think of as the Rule of Three Trips exists in part because not only can't the new fixture be fastened to hardware that held the old one, but at least one other system of installation has come and gone in the meantime, so that parts meant to adapt new fixtures to old systems (or old systems to new fixtures) do not fully bridge the gap. (If you think logic indicates that this situation should result in at most two trips to the hardware store, you are free to think what you like, but Uncle Al would like to bet against you.)

Recently, however, as a one-week vacation neared and he contemplated accomplishing various tasks around the house, Uncle Al realized that the Rule of Three Trips had emerged from projects that were largely—if not entirely—undertaken on weekends.

Perhaps, Uncle Al thought, that rule comes into play at least partly because of the need to complete such weekend projects rapidly—so some weekend time remains for catching up on taped *Rockford Files* reruns and shopping for Little Debbie Nutty Bars—and that this pressure might produce hasty and injudicious decisions that result in unnecessary hardware store visits.

If a whole week were available, Uncle Al thought, maybe the resulting deliberate, thoughtful, reasoned approach to such a project might result in completing it in only two hardware-store trips—or maybe even only one.

So it was that Friday night, at the beginning of his vacation, Uncle Al made a list of tasks he planned to accomplish in the following days. The less said about that the better, because nothing he did all week appeared on that list (but that's neither here nor there, and Uncle Al brings it up only to be honest).

By Saturday morning it had become clear to Uncle Al that his No. 1 task for that day, well above anything on his list (even though it was less pressing than everything on his list), was going to be rerouting the drain pipes under his kitchen sink.

To prevent momentary or extended loss of consciousness among his more delicate readers, Uncle Al will forgo a detailed discussion of the many steps involved. But he feels he owes those who would have stayed awake at least an outline of the problem.

It followed his installation several years ago of a new deep double kitchen sink with a garbage disposal on one side.

He had followed the disposal's installation instructions to the letter. Water from the disposal entered the drainpipe of the other tub from the side, and that pipe emptied into a single trap, from which everything was supposed to flow through the wall behind the sink and be heard no more.

Although in some sense everything worked, not all of the

ground-up output of the disposal went down the drainpipe. Often some portion instead splashed *up*, into the strainer of the other tub, necessitating frequent rinsing and swabbing to remove melon purée and worse.

Uncle Al called the disposal manufacturer and verified that he had correctly understood the recommended drain arrangement. But it was not wonderful, so over time he peeked under numerous other sinks (and at other disposals' installation instructions in stores) to see what he might have done wrong or how the installation might be improved. Most seemed to duplicate his own unsatisfactory arrangement, although they seemed to work better.

Looking back over the last painful week, Uncle Al realizes that he might have solved his problem simply by moving the pipe from the disposal so that it entered the other tub's drainpipe a little lower. That way the occasional particularly energetic burst of melon purée couldn't splash all the way up to the other tub's sink strainer.

But that is not what he did.

As it happens, a few months ago he came upon a couple of differently plumbed sinks. If he had followed their arrangement to the letter, that letter would have been Y: Each tub of those sinks had its own trap, and both traps fed into a Y-shaped pipe, the stem of which went into the wall behind the sink.

This appealed mightily to Uncle Al, because for any melon purée to turn up in the other sink tub's strainer under this configuration, it would have to go through the trap under the disposal, out to the Y near the wall and then, rather than going through the wall and off to never-melon land, some of it would have to turn around and go back into the other pipe and through its trap before it could splash up into the unoffending sink strainer. That sure wasn't likely to happen.

So the first Saturday morning of his vacation, Uncle Al set about to craft that Y-based arrangement out of easily as-sembled plastic drainpipe.

With a week and more available for the project (the July 4th holiday providing extra leeway), would the Rule of Three Trips still hold sway? Uncle Al really hoped not.

To bring this tale to its end with merciful swiftness, the Rule of Three Trips was indeed broken, but not the way Uncle Al expected. Over four days (interspersed with other fully pointless activity), the #@$% project took seven trips to the hardware store. The reasons can't easily be spelled out except to note that one shape of plastic fitting is no longer available with a particular kind of connection.

It used to be available, because Uncle Al's basement hard-ware collection had yielded one such piece, but Uncle Al needed two—one for each tub—and a tour of four hardware stores (which Uncle Al counted as one trip) yielded none. As a result, one drain and its trap looked fine; the other one was finally cobbled together with four right-angle bends.

It actually worked all right, but it looked so stupid that Uncle Al knew that if he ever wanted to sell his house, the first thing some inspector would require him to do would be to replumb the sink.

Therefore, with clarity of mind and purpose gained from four days of increasing familiarity with the available shapes and connectability of plastic fittings, on the fifth day Uncle Al removed the offending network of pipes and connectors and put together a substitute for the apparently obsolete item from some pieces of a different size plus some adapters. He accomplished the final (fairly decent looking) arrangement with only one additional trip to the hardware store.

That's a total of eight.

The pile of miscellaneous plastic fittings thus made useless now constitutes the 1999 Uncle Al Plumbing Collection, which occupies pride of place in his basement (near where the funnels used to be).

On the sixth day, Uncle Al considered hanging a new light fixture, but thought better of it and instead made a mess of beginning one of the least-important projects on his list.

On the seventh day, Uncle Al rested, watched tapes of *Rockford Files* reruns, ate Little Debbie Nutty Bars and cantaloupe, and tore up his list of projects.

But when he put the cantaloupe rind through the garbage disposal, the other tub of his sink remained free of melon purée.

It had been a good week.

Waiting for the Perfect Moment

ᵡᵡᵡ

Uncle Al has been feeling somewhat off his game lately.

He didn't realize quite how far he had slipped until a recent gathering at work, at which, he had heard, a colleague would be getting rid of some extras from a basket of olde-timey candy she'd bought for her husband's birthday. He pictured wax lips, chocolate cigarettes and those little barely flavored pastel sugar disks called Necco wafers.

Although he hadn't loved Necco wafers, Uncle Al remembered them for two reasons:

As a child he was amused to learn that the name Necco came from the candy's maker, the New England Confectionery Co.

And for almost all his adult life—since 1964, when he was 23—he'd been waiting to be offered a Necco wafer so that he could make a swell joke based on the slogan of Barry Goldwater's presidential campaign.

In the intervening years, both Necco wafers and the Goldwater campaign had receded from public awareness, so it was getting to be very unlikely that Uncle Al would ever be offered a Necco wafer, much less in a large-enough group that somebody present might remember the Goldwater slogan.

Then a few days ago, as noted, out of nowhere that perfect moment arrived: A crowd of his coworkers, of varied ages, stood around a table on which was arrayed the aforementioned assortment of candy, including a roll of Necco wafers.

Uncle Al espied the roll with pleasure, even examining it to verify that it was still produced by the New England Confectionery Co. But inexplicably, although at least 10 minutes went by as Uncle Al and others chatted, as people will, of love and life and the pursuit of inexpensive refreshments, at no point did the cobwebs in Uncle Al's brain drift aside sufficiently to fire the Necco joke synapse.

Had his mind been engaged, he wouldn't have waited very long to be offered a Necco wafer: Knowing that this was almost certainly going to be his last chance, he would have picked up the roll as though it had been offered, shaken his head sadly, and said, "No, thanks; I want a choice, not a Necco."

Half an hour later, he suddenly remembered, leapt to his feet, and hurried back to the table. Almost everyone had left, but a few stragglers were still there, and so were the Neccos, so Uncle Al gave it a shot, but his heart wasn't in it; it was a pitiful moment, nobody even looked up, and he slunk away, defeated.

It would have been better if the whole thing had never happened—if he had gone to his grave still waiting for the moment for "a choice, not a Necco," instead of knowing that after almost 42 years of burnishing it in his mind, he had mentally snoozed right through his only opportunity to use it.

As it was, he could picture the rest of his life unfolding like that of the guy in a *New Yorker* story he'd read a few years ago, a man driven completely around the bend—not by failing, as Uncle Al had, to use his cherished remark the first time it had been possible in decades, but by springing it on a crowd that he mistakenly thought had set it up:

"Personally, I think Angela Thirkell is a thquare" might have been funny if someone at the cocktail party had just mentioned

Angela Thirkell. Nobody had. And the pitying looks he got so deranged the poor fellow that he entered into a life of crime, in which he not only made up dreadful lines like that but spent years engineering situations in which he could say them.

(Uncle Al would love to credit the author of that story, but, astonishingly, he can't at the moment locate his copy—it might be with his funnels. If he ever finds it, he'll let you know.)

It is Uncle Al's hope, anyway, that this public admission of his failure in the Necco matter, in effect burning the letters N-E-C-C-O into his brow, will help him avoid a similar terrible spiral into depravity.

As his own reminder of this shameful defeat, he took the Necco wafers with him.

Next day, staring glumly at the roll on his desk, and there being nothing else handy to feed his sweet tooth, Uncle Al popped one into his mouth. It was better than he remembered.

But he really would rather have had a choice.

Note: Mark Storry, an alert reader in Monticello (at least he's more alert than Uncle Al), sent him the answer to the mystery of the *New Yorker* story a few weeks later:

The author of "Turtletaub and the Foul Distemper" was baseball writer Roger Angell; it appeared May 30, 1970. No wonder Uncle Al couldn't find it: Wherever it is, it's under almost as much life-rubble by now as his Goldwater "A Choice, Not An Echo" button.

Losing the Way to the Will

ᵔᶜᶜᶜ

Today's tale is a long one; sorry about that. And it's another indication that I'm not in full-time possession of my steel-trap mind. Admit it: You love to read about how other people are losing it.

First I have to explain a few things about my father. Until late last year, Dad was, as he would say, "in pretty good condition for the condition I'm in." At 95 he was living by himself in a small apartment in Milwaukee, doing his own cooking and responding to most situations with the same corny lines he was using when I was growing up. (The same lines I use.)

He didn't hear well, and he didn't see well, but he laughed pretty well, and he enjoyed television and cigars. Especially cigars.

For the last many years my father almost always had a cigar, not always lit, in one hand. Lots of family pictures are obscured by a blurry V—Dad's fingers, holding a cigar beneath the camera lens.

But when I was growing up, he tended to reserve cigars for somewhat special occasions, moments of small—but distinct—self-indulgence: after dinner; on an evening walk; on a Sunday morning.

The aroma of his cigar—from the living room, at a picnic, drifting over the lawn from his chair on the porch—was an announcement that my father was taking his ease. All through my childhood, that occasional scent of cigar smoke was my reassurance that, for the moment anyway, a little part of the world was OK.

I haven't been around my dad all that often since I moved to Minneapolis 30 years ago, but in that curious way that smells evoke pieces of memory, whenever I catch a whiff of cigar smoke, no matter where I am something inside me relaxes—something that I didn't even know was tense.

After Dad's vision got weak, the ash end of his cigar would bump into almost everything in his life, and most of his possessions began to carry at least a thin film of cigar ash. He didn't see it, of course, and if pushed he'd probably say that he liked the smell.

My niece, his granddaughter Kathy, took him grocery shopping once a week, and he bought her breakfast beforehand or lunch afterward. She and the woman who periodically cleaned his apartment made sure that the ash deposits were never too deep.

A couple of years ago Kathy and I sat Dad down to talk about his will, which he hadn't changed since before my mother died more than 20 years earlier. We also pressed him to look at a few nursing homes, so if that move became necessary we would know which ones he liked—or at least which ones he hated less than the others.

He did draft a new will, naming me executor and sole beneficiary, and telling me to take care of Kathy, but he washed his hands of the nursing home issue. "There's no rush, is there?" he asked. "I'm still buying green bananas."

I typed up the new will when I got back home, and sent it to Kathy. She got it signed, witnessed and into his safe-deposit box.

One morning last December, Dad fell in his bathroom and

broke his hip. I had gotten him one of those "I've fallen" buttons not long before, and surprisingly he hadn't balked at wearing it. It got him to the hospital in half an hour. (From the hospital he told me that he still thought it was too expensive.)

I went to Milwaukee, my son Dave was there for winter break, Kathy was on break from her job as a grade-school teacher, and everybody was able to see Dad. He was getting over a little lung congestion before the hip surgery was to be scheduled when he developed a blood clot, then a stroke, and he died.

It was a pretty good life, and, I guess, a pretty good death; he didn't suffer much and we all got to say goodbye.

After the funeral Kathy and I packed up his things. Except for cigar ashes, his papers were in very good order. Before I went back to Minneapolis, we got his will out of the safe-deposit box.

Dad's estate wasn't big. It consisted of the remnants of some stock my mother inherited in the '40s. Some of the stock was not terrific; Cuban Cane Sugar, for example, was no longer a big income producer. But when it was all sold, Kathy would get enough money for a down payment on a house—if the estate didn't get divided among folks Dad hadn't seen in years, as it would if we hadn't updated his will.

I learned immediately that it wasn't going to be that easy; I couldn't be executor because I'm not a Wisconsin resident. Kathy could, but it was going to take a while to straighten it out. So on my next trip to Milwaukee, Kathy and I put the stock back in his safe-deposit box.

I explained to her that even if she were to be the executor, I would do the work. Besides wanting not to burden her, I had another motive: Because she's a teacher, her apartment is always awash in paper. As a result, sometimes she loses track of stuff, and I would feel better if I stayed in charge of things.

After a few weeks I got in touch with the probate folks in Milwaukee, who said that we could walk the will through without an attorney if we got the other relatives to OK it. They said I had to go over the process in person, so one day in early February I went to Milwaukee.

I was told I wouldn't need to bring the will along. Before I left, though, I thought to myself, "This isn't smart, letting this valuable document sit out on my bureau. It's not valuable to anyone else, but it would be a problem if it were lost. I should get a safe-deposit box. In the meantime I should put this will somewhere less obvious."

I remember that moment with great clarity: I am standing in my bedroom, the will in my left hand, thinking, "I should put this somewhere." And that's the last thing I remember about it.

A few days after I got back from the probate-explanation trip to Milwaukee, I decided to begin the task, and I went up to my bedroom to get the will.

Which I couldn't find.

I spent the evening going through drawers, looking under things, and generally trashing the room. No will.

I decided that I must have put it in the other upstairs room, which I laughingly call my office and which is filled with bags of paper; I'd find it tomorrow night.

But I didn't. Nor did I find it in the next many days, as I got progressively more and more nuts trying to figure out where I might have put it. A friend suggested that it had to be in one of my two upstairs rooms because I must have put it away quickly—I would remember, for example, going all the way down to the basement with it. (Yes, faithful readers; just on the off chance, I searched the basement area where I keep funnels. It wasn't there.)

But my friend's analysis made sense, so I ripped the two upstairs rooms apart. Again. Nope.

I began to despair. If I had hidden the will, not just put it away somewhere, it was as good as gone. (Although I had lived in this house more than a year, the basement consisted mostly of piles of boxes still packed from the previous move or moves.) If I had cleverly put the will in the sixteenth book down in the box of 1964 computer wiring manuals (they're fascinating!), which is under four other boxes behind the main pile of boxes, I would never find it. (But it would be *really* safe.)

As days went by, I involved more and more of my friends in the problem, but I didn't tell Kathy: Why bother her until I knew for certain?

After several weeks of looking, I got a brilliant idea and had myself hypnotized to aid my recall. It didn't work, but I have to say that it was very relaxing.

So I kept tearing my house apart. In the process I discovered an awful lot of great hiding places. The will wasn't in any of them, but I decided that sometime I could write a book of great hiding places.

I agreed one Saturday to the offer of two friends to ransack the second floor of my house. I was banished to the basement so that I couldn't keep saying, "I looked there." We had a nice breakfast first, but that was all that happened.

On Sunday, I screwed my courage to the sticking point, as they say in British novels, and called Kathy.

"It's going to be a while before anything happens on the will," I said. "I can't find it."

"It's in the safe-deposit box here," she said.

"No it's not," I answered. "We put the stock back in the safe-deposit box, but I took the will with me to Minneapolis and I had it in my bedroom almost a month later, but now I can't find it."

"I saw you put it in the safe-deposit box," she said. "I don't have school next Friday. I'll go to the bank then and get it. I wish you had told me you were looking for it."

I decided not to argue with her because this way she was happy; if I convinced her that it was lost, we'd both be miserable. I felt too stupid to say I knew I had kept it because I'd been afraid she'd lose it.

On Friday, she called me at work.

The will, she said, was in the safe-deposit box in Milwaukee, just as she'd said it was.

I immediately called everyone I had dragged into this to tell them the good news: I hadn't irretrievably hidden the will; it was in Milwaukee all the time.

Linda, one of my nastier friends, observed, "Great! Now we know you're not stupid, just senile."

Even I saw the humor, so I told another friend, "I called Linda to tell her the good news, and she said . . ."

I had forgotten what Linda said; I had to call her back.

I drove to Milwaukee to get the will, and on the drive back to Minneapolis I stopped for lunch and locked my keys in my pickup truck. With the lights on. When I broke into the (locked) camper top to fish out the magnetic case that contained a spare key, it was empty. But otherwise things went OK.

I have many copies of Dad's will now, and the original is in a safe-deposit box in Minneapolis. I say that not only to indicate that I've learned my lesson, but also in case I forget where I put it—400,000 readers can drop me a line.

Meanwhile, I should have known all along that it wasn't in my house. The whole time I was looking for it, I never smelled cigars.

Goodbye, Dad.

Rollin' in the Flivver

ᴄᴄᴄ

Every once in a while one of my many unpleasant experiences leaves me uncertain about whether it was so bad that it spoiled my day or was so much better than it might have been that I'd really finished way ahead.

As do so many of my stories that seek to explore the more remote corners of human nature, this one involves my truck. (As Click—or maybe it was Clack—one of the Tappet Brothers, anyway—once observed: "We don't like cars; we like people. The cars are only . . . a vehicle!")

My truck is a 14-year-old mini-pickup that, although it has seen better days, is still quite serviceable. In fact, it is so serviceable that chances are excellent that at any given moment it is being serviced.

Not long ago I took it in to my regular place to have the brakes looked at, as they had become pretty lumpy-feeling. The folks there, who do very nice work, also fixed the parking brake, which hadn't worked since I bought the truck, used, many years ago.

Given that it has had no parking brake, I've always been very careful to park the truck in gear with the wheels turned in toward the curb, and it hasn't been a problem. But I'm planning to keep the thing another 20 or 30 years, so fixing the parking brake probably was a good idea.

The only time a nonfunctioning parking brake is a problem is on very cold days, when it would be nice to start the truck and let it warm up a little in neutral while I am somewhere warm.

Being able to do that also would help combat the interior frost that appears when I am foolish enough to exhale inside the truck before the defroster really warms up. But leaving the truck in neutral without a parking brake means that if the ground is not level, the truck rolls.

(You know where this is going, don't you? If I had visualized the situation as the beginning of a column, I would have known too. But sometimes a cigar is just a cigar.)

One cold morning about a week after the brake repairs, I got in and started the truck, then got out and scraped the windshield. In driving the first couple of blocks, to the place where I always stop to get a cup of coffee, I was having my usual problem keeping the windshield clear. But I realized that now that I had a parking brake, I could set it and leave the engine running while I bought my coffee. It would be only a minute, but that might give the defroster a chance to get a leg up (so to speak) on the windshield.

Without a parking brake I had never been able to leave the engine running there before, because the coffee shop's parking lot slopes—ever so gently—toward the street.

(Yes, I know you know what's coming. Don't spoil the surprise for others who aren't as bright.)

When I came out of the coffee shop, the truck was gone.

It wasn't like what had happened to me a few months ago at a shopping center, when I couldn't find my truck among the acres of cars, and I spent half an hour walking up and down the same four aisles (because I knew I had parked in an aisle that ended close to the door), trying to decide whether I should call the police. I didn't call them right away because I knew it was awfully unlikely that anybody would steal a truck like mine. It turned out I had come out the wrong door.

Anyway, it wasn't like that. The coffee shop has only one door, the parking lot is very small, and it was completely empty.

When I glanced up, however, there was my truck at an angle straddling the sidewalk—on the other side of the very busy street!

I ran over, dodging cars, to see what horrible damage it had caused to what other objects.

None! It had rolled across a heavily traveled street, in rush hour, without hitting another car, a pedestrian, a bicyclist or a building. It was stopped by a parking-lot curb. As far as I know there hadn't been so much as a horn honked at it. I felt immense relief that nothing horrible had happened to anyone.

Given the other possibilities, it would have been OK with me if the truck had been damaged, but it was fine, too—or as fine as it had been recently.

By coincidence, a colleague who lives nearby had been shopping at the bakery whose parking lot the truck had rolled over to. She had recognized the oddly parked truck, and as I crossed the street she was coming up to the door to see if I had keeled over dead in the seat.

No such luck, but I felt pretty close to it as I drove, somewhat shakily, to work. I tested the parking brake in the parking lot. It works fine; I must not have engaged it fully.

When I got to my desk, I told a few folks about what had happened. After I finished I still didn't know how I felt: It was a very bad start to the day, but it could have been a million times worse.

I don't know why I felt it necessary to decide how I felt, but

I did, and I couldn't. Maybe it would have been a good idea to convene a panel of optimists and pessimists and let them fight it out. Or maybe, I thought, I should take my own suggestion and say that my truck contained four ounces of water.

To my relief, I realized several days later that there was another aspect of the situation, forgotten at the time, that pushed the experience as a whole quite definitely into the positive column:

When I climbed back into the truck that morning and drove it off the sidewalk, the windshield was nicely defrosted.

Not Etching to Please

Uncle Al has done his share of mocking the stupid warnings that have been turning up on products: "Remove cardboard sun-shade from windshield before driving." "Do not operate electric mixer in bathtub." And he has had plenty of company in mining this source of amusement.

But somehow the more perverse cousin of the stupid warning—the impossible instruction—has escaped media attention.

By way of illustration, Uncle Al refers to notes he made last fall, when his new garage was just completed.

What we will call the Saga of the Concrete Sealer began when the bill for the completed garage arrived. Enclosed was a notice that the concrete floor must be painted with a particular sealer to protect it from oil and water, subsequent cracking and worse.

Uncle Al immediately bought the sealer and found that the instructions on the can said that the concrete must cure for 90 days before using the product. Fair enough. Uncle Al waited as long as he could, noting also the second instruction—to apply the sealer when the temperature is above 40 degrees.

The two requirements passed each other one weekend day in late October, and Uncle Al swept the garage floor in anticipation of painting it a bit short of the required 90 days but at least above freezing, before he read further down the can:

The concrete surface must be etched with acid, then rinsed

with water several times and allowed to dry a day or two before applying the sealer. After which, the instructions went on, the surface should not be driven on for three days.

The whole point of having a garage, besides storing Uncle Al's ever-growing pile of junk, was to store his lovely 1975 Chevy convertible, which is not yet rusting. But by the time he read about the need to etch the floor with acid two days before sealing it and five days before storing the car, it was starting to snow. He knew in his heart that city crews would be spreading salt out there any minute.

The instructions continued that if an automobile must be stored on the sealer after only 24 hours, a sheet of plastic should be put under each tire.

OK; that was it. Uncle Al had had enough.

There would be no acid, no rinsing, no waiting five days. He painted the floor with sealer as soon as he was done sweeping it. He waited only until the next morning to park his car on it, and he didn't put down any plastic sheets.

Uncle Al must admit that, even if the whole deal had begun in June, with plenty of warm weather ahead, chances are he would have decided anyway not to etch his garage floor with acid. In fact, he's pretty sure, even with all the time in the world, he would no more choose to spend a weekend etching his garage floor with acid than he would tasting all the fuzzy things from the back of his refrigerator to see which ones were really spoiled.

No, even to keep the sealer from peeling he would rather not deal with rubber gloves, fumes, acid pooling in the garage or in the alley (or flowing into the sewer), utensils he wouldn't know how to dispose of (probably including the good shoes he would have forgotten to change out of), and heaven knows what else.

When spring arrived this year, of course, Uncle Al found that a good deal of the sealant paint had flaked off, including all of it that had been under the car tires.

The point is not that sealant paint is flaking off of Uncle Al's garage floor. It's that he didn't for a moment even consider complaining to the store or the manufacturer, because he knew he hadn't followed the instructions on the can.

And if the garage floor begins to crack, he knows he needn't bother calling the contractor, who will ask whether he followed the instructions about sealing the floor.

Uncle Al doesn't really doubt that the sealer would have adhered better had he etched the floor first. But he does doubt that most people happily etch their garage floors with acid before painting them, and he thinks it's possible that there are sealant paints that wouldn't require etching.

In sum, he has a deep suspicion that some complex instructions are there in part to *guarantee* that they won't be followed.

Sure, probably there are some people out there swabbing acid around their garage floors every chance they get. They probably also do all three or four steps of "surface preparation" called for on cans of household paint, every one of which Uncle Al finds impossible. (If he could remove all the grease and whatever from his kitchen cabinets, for example, he wouldn't need to paint them in the first place.)

Those people also no doubt spend two hours reading the entire Internet service provider contract before they check "Accept."

Uncle Al is glad there are such folks, just to keep the concrete sealer companies honest, but for himself he thinks life is too short.

Now, if he could just figure out how to use his electric mixer while he's in the bathtub . . .

Soap Is Too Soon Parted

ᴖ ᴖ ᴖ

If you watch television at all you've seen the ads for Lever 2000, "for all your 2,000 parts." (Well, maybe you haven't seen the ads if you watch only public television and the aviation weather map, but that makes you kind of a special case.)

But even though you've been exposed to the ads, you might not have paid them much attention, so let Uncle Al refresh your memory before he proceeds:

Lever 2000 is a cleansing product, available both as a bar of soap and as a bottle of "antibacterial body wash," which Uncle Al believes to mean that it is . . . how to put it? . . . Soap. Liquid antibacterial soap.

Uncle Al will leave it to you to judge whether the liquid product is technically soap, since it consists not of the familiar sodium tallowate but instead is made of water, cocamidopropyl betaine, sodium cocoyl isethionate, dimethicone, sodium laureth sulfate, fragrance, ammonium sulfate, laureth-4, laureth-23, carbomer, mica, titanium dioxide, guar, hydroxypropyltrimonium chloride, sodium hydroxide, BHT, methylchloroisothiazolinone, methylisothiazolinone, and the active ingredient triclosan. (It also "may contain" propylene glycol—perhaps it does only on days when you've been nice and Lever feels like tossing in a little something extra.)

In any case, let's just call it soap, OK?

The ad points out that your body has many parts (it refrains from naming them, a practice that perhaps Uncle Al should have emulated with regard to the components of soap or body wash), and it goes on to note that this stuff, whatever it is, will clean them. And that's about it.

Thus I was unprepared when a colleague came to my desk bearing a bottle of Lever 2000 and indicated the orange flag on the front label that reads, "Over 70 uses." Besides washing with it, he wondered, what uses are there?

We discussed the matter briefly. I noted that if the folks at Lever Bros. were counting things like washing your elbow as different from washing your ankle, then supposedly there are 2,000 uses. And if they weren't counting washable parts separately, then I could think of washing, bathing, showering, laving, ablution, and other synonyms, but certainly not 70 of them.

Maybe they mean it can wash things besides yourself, such as your car, your air conditioner, and your barbecue grill. Or maybe Lever 2000 does other things than wash: Perhaps it frees stuck-on lug nuts, forms a flexible bond around dentures, and makes a delicious pie filling.

Clearly, the only thing to do was to call Lever Bros. and ask them for the list of 70 uses. I didn't know whether they had a list that they mailed out to pests like me or whether I would get transferred to a public-relations vice president who would explain that there were lots of uses for Lever 2000 and that 70 was only a fanciful estimate. Or maybe I would learn that this was the teaser for a contest to come up with 70 uses.

I did not expect the answer I got, nor did any of my friends anticipate it when I showed them the bottle of soap with its "Over 70 uses" claim.

"I have a bottle of Lever 2000 antibacterial body wash," I

told the woman who answered at Lever's consumer center, "and it says 'Over 70 uses.'"

"Yes," she encouraged.

"What are they?"

"What?" she asked.

"What are the 70 uses?"

"Oh!" she giggled, clearly surprised. She then explained, patiently, that the bottle holds enough to use it 70 times.

Well!

If my friends and I didn't understand it, there probably are millions—well, surely thousands—definitely a couple dozen—other folks who will find "Over 70 uses" confusing.

The problem, as I came to view it when I tried to explain to others what that phrase is supposed to mean, is that the term commonly employed in this regard comes from food packaging: "Over 70 servings" seems inappropriate when describing soap.

One friend offered a slight modification that might work: Serves 70. That seems to suggest 70 people all at once, however, and for most of us that situation arises only occasionally. And in fact, the bottle might well serve more like 140 if the occasion were more social than hygienic.

Perhaps the label should say "Serves one person 70 times."

Or maybe it should just say "soap."

Leapfrog Revisited

ˇᴄˇᴄ

I must apologize in advance for beginning today's effort by retelling a tale from a long-ago column.

I seem to be retelling a fair amount lately. I must say, however, that I do so not because I'm lazy—well, not *only* because I'm lazy—but also because I think a new development is more amusing when seen in its historical context. For example, I think somebody getting hit in the face with a cream pie is much funnier if we know that the same person previously lost a bundle investing in a cream-pie factory.

So please recall a cold day in . . . no, a cold day in February 1992, when I found myself with both a car and a truck I needed to get home (a mile or so away), and the car couldn't be shut off because its battery wouldn't be able to restart it.

So I drove the car two blocks, walked back and got the truck, drove it four blocks, walked back and got the car, drove it four blocks, walked back and got the truck, and so on. In effect, I walked home once and drove home twice. By the time I got home it was dark, and I went to bed. Some days you should just stay there.

OK. It's 5½ years later, I am infinitely wiser, and one day last week I came out of the newspaper building after work and found that my new ancient car—a 1975 Chevrolet convertible— wouldn't start. The battery was almost dead.

I knew at a glance what had happened: The day had been very nice, and I had driven to lunch with the top down. When

I got back from lunch and pushed the button to raise the top, it balked partway up, as it has tended to do sometimes recently. I need to fix that. For now, lifting up on the front of the very heavy top, while the button is pushed, gets it past the sticking point.

Unfortunately, a single person—or even a married one if temporarily unaccompanied—cannot simultaneously press the button, which is on the dashboard, and lift the top, which is behind the back seat when it sticks.

So I carry in the trunk a long, thin piece of lumber that I can use to press the button on the dashboard while I am standing in the back seat, lifting the top. I got it out and used it. Bingo.

Besides putting the top up, it is, of course, necessary to raise the windows when leaving a car, and these electric windows don't work unless the ignition is on. So I turned it on and raised the windows. Somewhere in there, I noticed that the trunk was still open and I returned the top-button stick to the trunk and closed it, fastened the clamps that hold the top in place, and went back to work.

Leaving the ignition—and the heater fan—on.

Many hours later I returned and found the battery on its last legs. It was fairly late—there must have been some Taste-section emergency, I don't recall what—but the only folks I know who park in that lot were already gone. I was pretty sure, however, that I had noticed another of my colleagues still at his desk when I left.

He parks in a lot about a block closer to the newspaper. (The newspaper has many employees and many parking lots: Employee parking is one of the newspaper's core businesses.) I walked over to his lot to make sure his car was still there, and walked back to the paper and up to the third floor to ask if I could borrow his keys to jump-start my car.

He gave me the keys; I went downstairs, walked to his lot, drove his car to my lot and jump-started my car. I knew I needed to give him back his keys, and I didn't want to leave my car with its engine running in the middle of an almost empty and fairly isolated parking lot. So, tremblingly aware that I must not turn off the ignition, I drove my car the couple of blocks to the building entrance, nervously left it idling near the door, went upstairs, thanked my friend, and gave him back his keys.

When I got back to my car (still there, still running, whew!), I realized that I had left his car over in my parking lot, hardly a neighborly thing to do when he had been so kind. So I decided to shuttle his car back to his parking lot. When I got to his car (in my car), I realized that in order to get his car to his lot, I would have to leave my car with its engine running in the middle of my lot—the same almost empty and fairly isolated lot I had rejected leaving it in moments before.

I was aware that I really hadn't enjoyed leaving my car idling outside the building entrance, either—just too big an invitation to theft for anybody walking by on the sidewalk— so I drove my car to his lot, somewhat busier and less isolated than mine, and I left it there idling. Then I walked back to his car in my lot, to get in and drive it to his lot . . . when I realized that I had already returned his keys.

So, with my car still idling in his lot, I walked back to the building from my lot—looking back several times on the way to check on my car in his lot. By the time I got back upstairs to get his keys to move his car from my lot back to his lot, I was very close to babbling. He graciously, and sensibly, suggested that I leave his car where it was and go home—that he could find it just fine in my lot.

Relieved, exhausted, and considerably the worse for wear, I left the building, went back to my car in his lot (still there, still running, whew!), and drove away.

By the time I got home it was dark, and I went to bed. Some days you should just stay there.

Americans Sort-of in Paris

ᶜᶜᶜ

Folks who peer into the future are scary. And even scarier is the happy new world that many of them see.

Public radio is lousy with such People with Vision. When there's nothing else to talk about, we in the commercial media have Madonna, RuPaul and the entertainer formerly known as Prince Charles; public radio has futurists.

I just heard an interview with Robert Ballard, the fellow from the Woods Hole Oceanographic Institute who found the sunken *Titanic* in part through the use of undersea remote-control robot TV cameras. Such robot cameras can be directed from a submarine or from a nearby surface ship.

In fact, Ballard said, he's actually looked in on those robots from his home. That was kind of interesting—satellite links to the ship and all that (and an indication that Ballard might not have a particularly active social life ashore)—but it wasn't enough to stop any listener in his or her tracks.

His next thought, however, was a concrete wall:

People are unable to use most of their time off for vacations, Ballard said, because most of it is on weekends, which are too short for lengthy trips. But we could eliminate that problem someday soon, he advised, by using TV robots and the Internet to cut transportation out of the vacation picture entirely:

Want to explore the high plains of East Africa? he asked rhetorically. Don't fly to Dar es Salaam; just dial up a TV robot at the speed of light. "In a quarter of a second," he said, "you're in the Serengeti."

(Either Ballard hasn't been correctly informed about the speed of light or he overestimates how far it is to Tanzania. It's roughly 8,000 miles, so at 186,000 miles per second it should take only about ¹⁄₂₄th of a second each way. Maybe he's allowing the other ¹⁄₈th of a second for dialing and the inevitable busy signals.)

In any case, Ballard envisions people all over the globe happily roaming everywhere they aren't, with the use of remote control robots.

"Billy! Nancy! Come down to the family room! Dad's about to take us to Paris for the weekend!"

"OK, everybody . . . just . . . dialing . . ."

Beep-bip-boop-boop-beep. Boorp-boop-hissssssss!

"OK, we're in. We're at the robot rental place near the Eiffel Tower. Let's walk over to the tower."

"Can we ride to the top, Daddy?"

"OK. Just a second here. I seem to be in the middle of a whole lot of robots. Aww. There's a long line of robots waiting for tickets. Let's come back later."

"That'll be fine, honey. Won't it, kids? That's an interesting-looking building over there. Let's walk that way."

"Sure. Oops! Yike! That %$#@ robot driving a Citroën almost knocked me down. What an idiot!"

"Look out for all those robots coming down the sidewalk, Daddy!"

"Oof. Hey, watch it, buddy!"

"Ah, oui? Vous êtes un . . ."

"He knocked us down, Daddy!"

"We need to get out of this crowd of robots, honey. Why don't we sit in a sidewalk café?"

"Good idea—here's one. I'll have to order something. Let's see what genuine French croissants look like."

"Monsieur, vous desirez . . ."

"(The waiter wants our order; I can do this.) Un café, s'il vous plait, et un croissant."

"Pairhaps ze gentleman inside ze robot would prefair to speak English; *zat* I could understand."

"(Smart aleck!) OK, a coffee and a croissant."

"Sank you."

"Look at all the robots going past, Daddy! And all the robots sitting at the café tables!"

"It *is* the height of tourist season."

"But where are all the people, Daddy?"

"At home, like us, enjoying their cyber-vacations."

" 'Ere is your coffee, Monsieur le robot Americain, and your croissant. Zat will be 18 francs. I don't suppose you 'ave any real money?"

"Uhh, no. Can you put it on my account? The robot has the number on his . . . uh, its . . . uh, my palm."

"Oui; sure; wizzout doubt. (Mumble, mumble. More papairwork, and probably no teep!)"

"Mom, that croissant looks real good. And look at all the fancy pastry in the window over there. Can we have some?"

"We're not really in Paris, kids. There's some leftover tuna salad in the refrigerator."

"Aww, Barb! Can't you make us something French?"

"Hey, lardbutt! It's my vacation, too. How about you and

the kids march the robot over to that McDonald's I see, and meanwhile I'll slip out and go to our McDonald's and bring back some real burgers."

"Good idea. And fries."

"*French* fries. You bet. I love travel; it's so broadening."

What Lane Is This Again? Oh, Memory!

ᴠᴠᴠ

Despite many experiences to the contrary, Uncle Al occasionally believes that something he has witnessed or thought of is so good or so bad or so funny or so weird (and therefore so ripe for his column) that he can't possibly forget it, so he doesn't need to write it down.

That belief is almost never correct, and it is mildly surprising to Uncle Al that he continues to come up with it.

Please understand: Uncle Al doesn't have a really bad memory. In fact, Uncle Al's memory probably isn't any worse than most people's; it's just that his need to recall specific things and his commitment to go to some length to commit specific things to memory seldom center on the same specific things—at least they don't do so at the same time.

In addition to that weakness, which Uncle Al suspects is not uncommon among people several decades past likely membership in the Britney Spears Fan Club, Uncle Al freely admits to having one narrow but deep memory flaw: For at least 15 years he has had a very hard time recalling proper nouns—not only names of people, but of places, books, movies and the like.

His other memory lapses (What was I going to buy at Target? Where are the funnels? Didn't I used to have another suit?) are random in kind and happen only occasionally. But he can almost count on being unable to fill in a proper noun when one is called for.

If he is having lunch with the same several colleagues with whom he has had lunch every weekday for several years, for example, and somebody else he knows equally well—but from another part of his life—turns up, so that introductions are in order, Uncle Al probably can't do them.

Uncle Al generally describes well-known Hollywood personalities something like this: He's that guy . . . ; he was in that movie . . . with that other guy . . . I think there's a B in his name. Or maybe not."

Uncle Al's friends are accustomed to this failing. In fact, his friends actually seem to enjoy Uncle Al being unable to come up with a name. When Uncle Al says something like "It's that guy," they start offering, unsolicited, rapid-fire lists of names, refining the scope of the list each time Uncle Al, a bit rattled by this performance, adds more clues.

If Uncle Al says, "I saw a guy on the street today who looked exactly like . . ." his friends start shouting "Adolf Hitler! Herbert Hoover! David Hasselhoff! Henry Kissinger!" until Uncle Al adds, "Not a politician; an actor. He was in that movie . . ."

"Tom Cruise! James Dean! Sidney Greenstreet! Harvey Keitel!"

"I think he sings, too. He . . ."

"Elvis! Kenny Rogers! Dean Martin! Gene Autry! Pat Boone! Sammy . . ."

Whereupon Uncle Al says, "That's it! Bob Hope!" and everybody grumbles.

Anyway, although he's not overwhelmingly convinced he needs help (except, perhaps, for that proper-noun problem), Uncle Al has been thinking for some time about trying ginkgo biloba, an herb that is said to have positive effects on memory. He decided a couple of months ago to give it a try.

The brand Uncle Al bought, after checking with his doctor, is supposed to be taken twice a day with food, and he easily added one ginkgo capsule to the couple of prescription drugs he takes every morning with breakfast.

But his dinner habits are somewhat irregular, and he takes no other medication in the evening, so he must admit that at first he was not very conscientious about taking that second ginkgo capsule. As a result, he wasn't sure he could expect significant results.

All that said, now that he is almost at the end of his second month of taking ginkgo, Uncle Al can report this single—but unequivocal—improvement in his cognitive functioning:

He regularly remembers to take his second ginkgo capsule.

Hard Charging into the Future

I like to think that I have been wise, over time, in making the occasional repairs that are required by the 1983 Ford Ranger pickup that I use for my daily transportation, instead of consigning it to the trash heap and buying a whole new (or more likely just a newer) vehicle.

You can pay for a great many $100 repairs, after all, before beginning to approach the monthly payments on a new (or newer) car. At least, that's how I have seen it. (I have also, incidentally, paid for a great many such repairs.)

So when, on my way home from work a couple of weeks ago, I killed the engine on the freeway entrance ramp and found, to my amazement, that I could not restart it because the battery was almost fully dead, it didn't even occur to me to let the battery's death rattle serve for the rest of the vehicle, too. I didn't even consider, after 240,000 miles, letting it join the host of other bygone pickups instead of being almost the lone '83 Ranger still out there slogging.

(Oh, all right; I know there are plenty of them. I just wanted to slip in that "lone Ranger" remark.)

Anyway, just as I started walking back up the ramp, my boss's boss pulled up in her shiny new car. We jump-started the truck and I drove off, deeply grateful.

I could see immediately, from many indications—dim lights, no turn signals, dashboard ammeter pointing the wrong way— that the battery was not recharging—that the alternator had ceased to alternate (instead of good-evil-good-evil, it was stuck on evil) and I knew that, wherever I stopped with the truck, it would not start again by itself.

The alternator must have gone out a while ago for the battery to get so low; I must have been preoccupied (maybe with the idea of chocolate-coating Marshmallow Peeps) not to have noticed that.

So, guilt aside, it was now 7 p.m. and I needed to decide where to take the truck. Several garages have ministered to it in recent years (increasingly so since its car mitzvah in 1996), but all would be closed, and none is so close to my house that it would be a snap to get home if I left it overnight. Yes, I could call friends to pick me up, but I was not sure that any of them were home.

If the weather had been a little warmer—and if I didn't need the truck to be running for an errand the next evening—and if I wasn't kind of tired—and if I hadn't already pictured having a nice warm dinner and watching TV—and if I could remember where I had put that old coat that I wouldn't mind getting greasy—I'm sure I would have considered fixing it myself.

That would have meant driving to a parts place, leaving the truck idling outside (hoping that the engine would not die—and that the truck would not roll away), buying an alternator, driving home, and staying up half the night getting cold and greasy and skinning several knuckles while installing it myself. I used to do lots of stuff like that. (Boy, am I glad I'm older now!)

As it was, I rolled slowly home, my path bathed in gold by my fading headlights, with my only thought being that I'd wait until the next morning to figure out what to do.

It wasn't until I pulled into my garage that I realized that I was facing a situation quite unlike the occurrences to which I have grown accustomed, in which I have two vehicles to move from one place to another and have had to play variations on the puzzle about the fox, the corn and the chicken, endlessly walking back and forth between them as I ferry the two from place to place.

Instead, in this case, I had a battery-dead vehicle, but it was parked right next to another vehicle (the lovely summer car, resting quietly until spring) that had a fully charged battery— and that I didn't have to move!

All I would have to do in the morning was jump-start the truck from the car battery and then drive to the nearest repair place. Better yet, I would cable the two batteries together overnight, giving the dead one a breath of life.

I enjoyed a warm dinner, watched TV all evening, and didn't look for my old coat.

Next morning, I found that in my haste to have a warm dinner, watch TV, and not look for my old coat, I had forgotten to cable the batteries together.

No problem. I did it then, started the truck, disconnected the cables and drove off, full of cereal and misplaced confidence, to a garage a few miles away—stopping first, of course, to get my usual coffee.

I carefully set the parking brake and made sure the engine was idling well before I went into the coffee shop. When I came out with my coffee, to my delight, the truck was still running.

So I got in and promptly killed the engine.

And the battery was still dead.

I should note that I have been driving cars with stick shifts since 1958. I almost never kill the engine. I was getting set to walk back to my garage, retrieve the other car from hibernation, drive it to the coffee place, jump-start the truck, drive the car back to my garage, and walk back to the truck (I don't know what there is about me that makes me particularly subject to that phenomenon), when one of the coffee-shop owners pulled up next to me and offered a jump.

That worked fine, although I was aware that there was no longer enough battery left to run the lights—so I'd better get where I was going before there wasn't enough to run the ignition—when it started to snow.

There wasn't enough battery to run the windshield wipers.

Luckily the snow stayed at the light-flurry stage long enough for me to get to the repair place, where I lucked out again: They had an alternator that fit. They also replaced, for good measure, a belt that had grown old in my service, as well as a voltage regulator whose terminals were withered by age.

While I waited, I explained to the woman who had become my waiting-room-mate that I saw no need to replace the fifteen-year-old truck despite its need for the occasional repair, because it was otherwise perfectly sound—except for things that, as I began to enumerate them, made kind of a long list.

When I got to the part about my having left the dashboard trim off because the radio is out being repaired—and that because removing the dashboard trim (with its colored lenses) left the warning lights blindingly bright, I had temporarily stuffed the area in front of each light with Kleenex—I sensed that she was no longer with me.

In fact, as I stopped before I got to the carburetor that needs replacing, I was beginning to wonder whether *I* was with me.

Just then a runner arrived with a replacement wheel for a customer's nice newish Audi. The one on the car had gotten bunged up. It was a very nice wheel—two mechanics came by to admire it—but it cost more than $200. For a wheel.

I started to think about how nice it is to have a vehicle on which I don't feel the need to spend anything—certainly not more than $200—if I scrape the curb with a wheel. Sure it's rusty; sure it's got an antifreeze leak; sure it needs a new carburetor.

But if I keep going the way I have, it won't be too long before I've replaced every part on it, so I'll have a whole new (or newer) vehicle. And how many people who have a new car can also say that, if they sneeze while they're driving, there's a whole bunch of Kleenex right in front of them?

Ghosting Downhill

ᶜᶜᶜ

The world of book publishing is peculiar indeed, but I thought I had a fairly clear handle on the concept of authorship: The author of a book is the person who wrote it.

True, there are "ghostwritten" books—where some person, usually a celebrity, is proclaimed as the author of a book really written by someone else. As a prime example of that genre, consider the stunning work *Comanche,* by margarine model Fabio "in collaboration with Eugenia Riley."

(The first two meanings of "stun" in *Webster's New World Dictionary* are "to make senseless or unconscious as by a blow" and "to daze or stupefy." It is in those senses of the word that *Comanche* was stunning.)

Fabio was gracious enough to acknowledge Riley's "contribution" in his dedication; after reading the book I thought he would have been better off claiming it had been all Riley's work and he'd obviously had nothing to do with it. But I digress.

In my endless search for truth, justice and clean restrooms, I have just come across what I believe to be a new kind of ghostwritten book—one in which some person writes a book that is allegedly written by a fictitious person, who is the main character in the book and who writes books.

I speak of *The Highland Fling Murders,* apparently the seventh book in the *Murder, She Wrote* series by Jessica Fletcher! That's right, Jessica Fletcher, a fictional character in a TV series, who writes mystery novels and solves crimes, is said to be the author of these mystery novels, in which she writes mystery novels and solves crimes.

I had the feeling that an endless hall of receding mirrors had opened in front of me, and I almost had to lean on Sid Hartman for support.

There is no scene in this book in which Fletcher relaxes by watching an episode of *Murder, She Wrote* on television, but there could be.

Donald Bain, said to be the ghostwriter of at least some of the Washington mystery novels allegedly written by Margaret Truman, plays the Eugenia Riley role here—his name appears on the cover next to Fletcher's—but in this case he also wrote the dedication. If only he had stopped writing at that point . . . But I digress again.

I don't know how I missed the other books in the *Murder, She Wrote* series, which include *Martinis & Mayhem, Rum & Razors, Manhattans & Murder,* and *Brandy & Bullets.*

Nor do I know why this one, which takes place in Scotland, was titled *The Highland Fling Murders,* and not *Scotch & Slaughter, Scotch & Slaying, Scotch & Shooting, Scotch & Suffocation, Scotch & Sleeping with the Fishes* or *Scotch & Sending Someone Prematurely to His or Her Final Reward.* Perhaps some association of Scotch whiskey distillers lobbied against that idea and traded Bain an evening in the Robert the Bruce bedroom in exchange for his going with *Highland Fling.*

Back to the main problem.

I acknowledge that books with fictional narrators are as old as papyrus, and that the names of such narrators have sometimes appeared as "authors" (including several new Sherlock

Holmes stories alleging to be recently discovered manuscripts by John H. Watson, M.D.). But a fictional narrator who is the author of the books in which she appears as the author of the books in which she appears is, I think, a new ball game.

Can it be taken even further—a fictional narrator who is the author of the books in which she appears as the author of the books in which she appears—as the author of the books in which she appears? (This would be, for example, a novel by Jessica Fletcher, in which Jessica Fletcher, who writes mystery novels and eventually solves a stabbing in Yellowknife, writes a book in which Jessica Fletcher writes mystery novels and eventually solves a hanging in Great Neck.)

Why not? Long, long ago, in the early heyday of *Mad* magazine, which ran very funny but possibly spurious letters to the editor, there was a letter to the editor that read as follows: "The guy who writes the letters to the editor should write the rest of the magazine."

Next month there was a letter to the editor that said "The guy who writes the 'The guy who writes the letters to the editor should write the rest of the magazine' letters should write the rest of the magazine." Next month there was "The guy who writes the 'The guy who writes the "The guy who writes the letters to the editor should write the rest of the magazine" letters should write the rest of the magazine' letters should write the rest of the magazine."

And so on, I think, for years.

Perhaps Jessica Fletcher could be seen thinking about killing somebody with a copy of her next Jessica Fletcher book, in which she is seen thinking about killing somebody with a copy of her next Jessica Fletcher book, in which she is seen thinking about killing somebody with a copy of her next Jessica Fletcher book, in which . . . and so on. It could be the entire text of the eighth book in the *Murder, She Wrote* series: *Murder with "Murder with 'Murder with "Murder with*. . . .

Scents and Sensibility

ᕁᕁᕁ

It's been quite a while since this column has concerned itself with something Lucky has said to me. Our most recent disturbing exchange is not a very long one, but it does indicate that Lucky has a fine appreciation for literary style.

We were out for a walk a few weeks ago, me doing not a whole lot of thinking about anything, when he stopped for the umpteenth time in two blocks to sniff at a tree before peeing on it.

I am told by those who pretend to understand animals' behavior that the latter act has to do with marking one's territory. Apparently the sniffing that precedes it has to do with checking out who has marked the territory previously.

One can hardly get upset at a dog for doing what dogs do, but when the dog is doing it on a cold, windy day, as this one was, one can get impatient—particularly if the dog insists on sniffing for what seems to be an excessive length of time.

The tree in question must have been especially interesting, because Lucky was sniffing it for at least a full minute while I kept wishing I'd worn a jacket. A minute isn't a lot of time on any reasonable scale, and it's not as if I had something lots better to do than stand there while he sniffed, but as the time wore on, my tolerance wore off.

"Come on, Lucky," I finally grumbled, tugging on his leash. "What could possibly be that fascinating?"

He responded immediately, without looking up from the tree: "Al," he said, "you have no idea."

As I thought about that on and off during the remainder of our walk, I realized that, in addition to my annoyance at how patronizingly he always uses my first name, I was annoyed because he was right, as usual.

I don't really follow sports, for example (an understatement on a par with "I don't often eat bald eagles"), but if pressed I bet I could write a few reasonably convincing paragraphs about the sensations and emotions felt by an NFL quarterback.

Similarly, I would not enjoy either witnessing or appearing in grand opera, about which I know almost nothing, but I believe that, if there was some reason to do so, I could make a pretty good stab at describing the appeal of opera to opera fans and to opera singers.

I might be wrong, and everyone who knows anything about football or opera might laugh themselves silly at my wildly misguided efforts, but at least I *think* I could do it.

But I literally have no idea what the sensations of extended tree sniffing are like for Lucky or what they do for him.

I gather that he's able to sort out, in some kind of dog-beezer urinalysis, who-all has been by lately to stake a claim on that territory, and maybe when, or what they've been eating or even whether they've been under some stress at home, but I can't imagine what that's like.

When Lucky sniffs a tree, is he reassured or aggravated to discover that Ralph up the block has been there again? Is there any pleasure in recognizing (if he does) that another of the tree's recent visitors had happened upon some leftover steak?

And, for that matter, quite apart from what they might signify, what are those aromas themselves like to him? Clearly they aren't unpleasant or he wouldn't want to experience them at such length, especially when I keep yanking on his neck because I forgot to wear a jacket.

If they convey anywhere near as much information about the tree's guest book as some experts tell us, they must be pretty complex.

That last thought came up near the end of our walk, after what seemed to me to have been a particularly egregious series of prolonged attempts on Lucky's part to inhale entire trees despite my almost continuous leash tugging.

It did seem as if the complexity of these aromas might be a facet of the topic I could get hold of, so when we were between trees I asked him. "Is it anything like what people write about wine tasting, Luck?"

"Yes it is, Al," he replied, "but it's far less pretentious."

I've got to stop leaving the Taste section lying around where he can see it.

A Mudsummer Night's Dream

Editor's note: *We can't seem to locate Uncle Al, but we found these notes for an utterly fictitious tale for children on his desk. Given how low our standards are for this column even when he is here, we haven't bothered to read it. We simply verified that it's long enough to fill Uncle Al's space. Enjoy.*

The Poor Couple Who Wanted Enough

Once upon a time, in a faraway kingdom, there lived a poor man and a poor woman and their 2.3 poor children.

All day the poor man sweated at a backbreaking job and the poor woman tended their mud hut and 1.3 of their poor children (the oldest poor child walked to school each day through miles of mud). In addition, the poor woman eked out a supplement to their income by selling get-rich-quick schemes on the Mudnet.

As the sun set each night the poor man would come home, tired from his long day of breaking backs, and fall into a chair. Presently, the poor woman would go "Eke!," having sold a get-rich-quick scheme, and she would get up from her work, clean up after the 0.3 of a poor child, who was (naturally) very messy, build a fire under a pot of mud, and begin to cry.

"Husband," she would wail, "will we never have enough?"

"What do you mean, Wife?" he said (for that was her name), knowing very well what she meant but hoping somehow each night that if he could only be kind enough and obtuse enough, he could somehow turn aside her sadness and be left to simply fall into chairs, which he had learned rather to enjoy. "We have enough poor children, surely," he said, "and enough . . . spoons . . ."

It was a very lame answer, and sometimes the poor man would say "forks" or "walls," just for variety.

At this the poor woman would look at her husband for a very long time.

Eventually she would speak: "It is not you who angers and saddens me, Husband. It is the System. If only we could invest some of the not-enough money that the king's foolish advisers in Capitolville hold for our old age, all the wealth we could earn would give us enough money for our old age—and maybe we wouldn't have to scrimp so much now! *Then* would life ever be sweet, hey!"

"Yes, Wife," the poor man would say, and he would go into the basement to sort mud.

One evening when the poor man came home the poor woman was waiting at the door. "Great news!" she shouted. "The king's foolish advisers have granted us a boon! One third of what had been set apart for our declining years we can now invest ourselves!"

"Hoo, boy!" said the poor man, and he and the poor woman promptly arranged to use that part of their meager retirement fund to buy a small part of one of the kingdom's most successful companies.

"They trade mud futures," a troll explained to the poor man and the poor woman. "It's all very complicated, but you can't argue with numbers like these," and he waved a piece of paper at them.

Truly, the poor man and the poor woman couldn't argue with the numbers, because they didn't know what the numbers meant.

And in fact, the numbers didn't really mean that, anyway.

For a while the poor man and the poor woman were happy. The poor man would come home, tired from his long day of breaking backs, and fall into a chair. Presently, the poor woman would go "Eke!," having sold a get-rich-quick scheme, and she would get up from her work, clean up after the 0.3 of a poor child, build a fire under a pot of mud, and tell the poor man: "We're up 37½ cents!"

The whole topic of "enough" stopped coming up. Sometimes, knowing how much wealth their investment would bring them in their old age, instead of scrimping they splurged on takeout mud for supper. They were very happy.

Then one evening (chair, "Eke," clean up, pot of mud), the poor woman told her husband nervously, "There are reports of various kinds of feasance at our company, including mal-, mis- and non-, to say nothing of dys-, hypo- and counter-. The head of the company has been deducting his lunch as a capital expense. We're down $2.50." The poor man and the poor woman began to worry.

The next day, they were down $3.12. And the next and the next, more of the same. And they worried a lot.

One day, when their whole investment was worth less than a single pot of mud, the poor man and the poor woman went to see the troll. There were many other poor people there, crowded at the troll's door.

The troll came outside with a megaphone and explained:

"It's all very complicated," he shouted. "But it will turn around. But you understood the risks of investing. But don't worry. But you know there's no free lunch. But the company is sound."

Then he went back inside.

The poor man and the poor woman went home and had half a pot of mud for supper.

Several days later the poor man and the poor woman learned that the company had closed, that there was nothing inside the building, that everyone who worked for the company was out of a job, and that the head of the company and the troll and a few of their friends had taken the money and run Venezuela.

"Oh, Husband," the poor woman cried, "now in our old age we will have only two-thirds of not-enough."

"Yes, Wife," the poor man said, "but now we can stop worrying about our investment." And he went into the basement to sort mud.

Going Door to Door

At some point I might well get tired of having a life that makes good fodder for a stupid column.

Perhaps I should have been able to avoid the mistake I made last weekend. Perhaps my awareness of the unpleasant possibilities inherent in what I was doing should have been raised by earlier nasty experiences. But that is not my way.

It's not that I repeatedly make the same mistake; I always try to achieve subtle variations on my previous mistakes.

It has been something like ten years since I managed to hit my old truck with my very old convertible and later the same day hit my very old convertible with my old truck.

And almost three years have passed since the winter that I left that truck running in a coffee shop parking lot, apparently not fully engaging its parking brake, and came back out to see it resting on the other side of the busy street, having miraculously hit absolutely nothing when it rolled over there.

The years fly on forever, and I still own an old truck and a very old convertible. They aren't the ones referred to above—each is a few years newer than its predecessor. OK, very few.

The convertible has a few things wrong with it—most of which hover tantalizingly just beyond my tinkerer's ability to fix them. So a week ago I spent a pleasant Sunday morning and early afternoon tinkering.

I took the driver's door half-apart to stop the window from rattling (taking the passenger's door similarly half-apart so I could see the difference), replaced the oil-fouled spark plugs on the two cylinders whose condition indicates just how much the whole engine needs to be rebuilt (and managed in the process to make the engine run a little rougher than it had before), and located and opened the clogged drain hole that had caused rainwater to pour into the car instead of onto the street.

I had parked the car half in and half out of the garage, so I had room to work but not in the bright sun, and I had the radio on to keep me company. By 2:30 or so, I was pretty well done in, but it had been a good day. I buttoned up the car, got in, and turned the key—and found that between the radio, the underhood light that comes on when the hood is up (which it was a lot), and the interior lights that come on when the doors are open (which they were a lot), I had run the battery down.

It wasn't all that heavy an electrical load. The battery must not have been in terrific shape to start with; I made a mental note to pick up a new battery sometime.

Meanwhile, no problem; the truck was out on the street nearby, and I had a good pair of jumper cables. I brought the truck around and nosed it in carefully on the right side of the convertible, which was not as far to the left of the door opening as it might have been had I expected to need to get the truck in there, too.

No problem, except that in snaking the truck into the narrow space I kept as close to the convertible as I could (to make sure that the passenger's side didn't scrape the garage door opening). That left no room to open the driver's side door of the truck; I had to get out of the truck on the passenger's side, first wriggling over the transmission lever and the dog's half-full water cup in the center console.

I connected the jumper cables and tried starting the convertible the easy way—without the truck engine running. Nope—not quite enough oomph there to overcome the long cables and imperfect connections at the batteries; I would need to start the truck's engine, to add the truck's alternator to the picture.

No problem, but the truck would need to be in neutral, with the parking brake on (because although the garage is only a couple of years old, and the floor is pretty level, there was always a chance that the truck could roll). I got in (on the passenger's side), reached my foot way over the transmission lever and the dog's water cup, and stepped on the parking brake. Then I pulled my leg back over onto the passenger's side (this whole deal is quite awkward), popped the transmission lever into neutral (that's very easy to do without stepping on the clutch), and turned the key.

The truck's engine started, apparently giving the truck just enough of a shake to make it recognize two things: The garage floor is level, but the back wheels were on the downward-slanting apron, not the floor; and the parking brake had not caught. (Yes, it's a different truck, but it, too, turned out to have a &¢%# parking brake that is easy to only partly engage.)

In what seemed like slow motion, the truck began to roll—unhurriedly but relentlessly—back out of the garage. Still in the passenger's seat, I attempted to pop the transmission lever back into gear to stop it (that's very hard to do without stepping on the clutch) and frantically reared back in the seat to begin the process of getting over to the driver's side so I could step on the brake. That's when I heard, to my right, a sickening noise.

The passenger's door, which of course I had left wide open, had encountered, flat on, the part of the garage wall next to the door opening. The door bent farther open than wide open, the top of the door bent some more, the window glass shattered, and—as I watched, frozen in place and half-expecting the garage wall to give way—the truck stopped.

It hadn't gone very far, nor gotten up much speed, so in hindsight it's not a surprise that the garage didn't collapse around me. But at the time it seemed like a close call.

I went into the house, got a drink of water, went back out to look at the mess, went back in, got another drink of water and called an auto parts recycler. He located a door at another auto parts recycler and said he could have it for me in a few days. (I would have said "junkyard," but I don't have the door yet, so I want to be as respectful as I can about this.)

Before he could order the door, though, he would need it to be paid for. No problem, I said, I'd drive right out.

Uhhh. Not with the truck, whose door was stuck wider than open inside the front wall of the garage. And not with the convertible, whose battery was dead.

Although the truck's resting place was probably perfectly stable, it was now too far away from the convertible for another jump-start. (The cables had pulled off—and somehow had the grace not to short-circuit the truck battery and maybe cause an explosion in the process.)

So I removed both batteries, installed the truck battery in the convertible, drove it out to the parts recycler, arriving minutes before closing time, paid for the truck door, and bought a new battery for the convertible.

Then I drove back home, put the new battery in the convertible, put the truck battery back in the truck, and muscled the door closed enough (bending the fender a little—or, to be accurate, a little more—in the process) to allow me to pull the truck forward so I could close the garage door behind it.

It hadn't occurred to me until the garage door closed that the incident might have pulled its track sufficiently out of line to prevent it closing. That hadn't happened. Small favors.

I can hardly wait for the weekend of attempting to install the replacement door. (I'm not going to rely on my own skills to fix the parking brake, but I think I might be able to handle the door job.) Stay tuned.

An acquaintance recently observed, after I described a much smaller automotive setback, that many people take their car problems to car-repair professionals.

Well, sure, but where's the fun in that?

What's the Antimatter Now?

An international team of physicists working with a 1.3-mile particle accelerator and a 1,200-ton detector at Stanford University announced that they have discovered a tiny difference between the behavior of a subatomic particle called a B-meson, and the behavior of its antimatter counterpart—a difference that they say might be the key in explaining why the universe didn't simply disappear in a flash of light as soon as it was created. —News item

Oh, those nutty physicists! Give them a 1.3-mile particle accelerator and a 1,200-ton detector and before you know it they start discovering that tiny things you never heard of have even tinier differences.

Uncle Al read several news reports about this discovery and is happy to offer this condensed explanation:

The Big Bang at the beginning of the universe 10 billion or 12 billion years ago (once you get within hailing distance of age 60, Uncle Al points out, a couple billion years here or there doesn't seem like such a big deal) created equal amounts of matter and antimatter. (Antimatter is stuff that is the opposite of matter: Anti-atoms contain such particles as anti-electrons, which are exactly the opposite of electrons, etc.; this is kind of like one of those everything-is-crazy alternate worlds in *Superman*, but not as amusing.) When matter meets antimatter, the two disappear, leaving only a burst of radiation (and perhaps a dry-cleaning bill).

Because that mutual disappearance should have left the universe empty after the Big Bang was done banging, physicists have been going around looking for 1.3-mile particle accelerators and 1,200-ton detectors with which to ferret out any slight differences in the decay of subatomic particles of matter and antimatter that would explain how a bunch of matter would have been left over after the Big Bang. (If it weren't for these tiny differences, they believe, the universe wouldn't exist, and it would then be very difficult to get funding for such a project.)

This new finding about B-mesons is the second such result (the first, that K-mesons and anti-K-mesons differ slightly, was announced 37 years ago), and scientists hope to find more such differences, because those two together account for only a billionth of the matter in the universe, a significant part of which is Adam Sandler.

Uncle Al hardly knows how to put this without appearing to minimize the vision of all those physicists, but he isn't sure that discovery of new differences between matter-antimatter pairs is needed to complete the picture of the origins of the universe.

The discoveries that explain the existence of one-billionth of the matter in the universe might, in fact, explain all of it, because of a second phenomenon (one that can be observed without even a two-foot particle accelerator): the increasing amount of matter in the universe.

Extrapolating from the stuff in his own basement and garage, Uncle Al would estimate that the amount of matter in the universe is doubling every 10 years. But because he is aware that his stuff might be doubling lots faster than the stuff of folks in sub-Saharan Africa and those on the Arctic tundra, for example, he has calculated how often, on the average, the amount of stuff in the universe would have to double in order for it now to contain a billion times what it did after the Big Bang ten billion years or so ago.

It would have to double only 30 times—once every 33 million years or so. Uncle Al's collections doubling every 10 years might be atypical for the whole universe, but surely even Siberians find they have twice as much stuff after 33 million years.

Just because he is having a good day, Uncle Al offers to the world of physics, free of extra charge (positive or negative), a second, and apparently unexplored, explanation of why matter was left after the matter and antimatter produced by the Big Bang noticed each other and went boom:

Maybe there weren't equal amounts of matter and antimatter in the first place.

Uncle Al, for example, always makes a little more gravy than is needed for the size of the turkey he serves. Mightn't the Big Bang have created a little more matter than antimatter, just to get the universe off the ground? (If not, there would never have been olestra potato chips, and wouldn't that have been a shame?)

None of the above was meant to imply that Uncle Al wasn't fascinated by the newest research. If nothing else, it renewed his interest in documenting the nature of anti-Uncle Al (from a safe distance, of course, so the two of him don't annihilate each other).

Some of the properties of anti-Uncle Al (also known as Auntie-Al, or Awntie-Al, depending on where you grew up) are obvious, given that they are exact opposites of the properties of Uncle Al: While Uncle Al is widely esteemed for his great wisdom, for example, Auntie-Al is notable for her athletic ability, her toughness under pressure, and for never looking like she slept in her clothes.

Auntie-Al works much more purposefully than the scatter-shot Uncle Al, thus she would have long ago finished the re-anti-carpeting job on her anti-convertible, but anti-time runs backward from time, so even now the areas of anti-rot on the anti-floor of her anti-convertible are changing back into anti-carpet, sparing her the trouble.

Similarly, Auntie-Al is at this moment pulling her fingers off of anti-keys on an anti-keyboard, causing patterns of anti-electron beams to recede from the glowing screen of an anti-computer monitor, erasing this very column.

Those who wish they subscribed to the anti-*Star Tribune,* so they would thus have been spared reading this column, are urged to recognize that many elements of the antimatter universe are less than pleasant:

- When you feel fine, for example, you take a biotic that makes you sick. Then you take a dote to get even sicker.
- Anti-Italian meals end with a big plate of pasto.
- And anti-ketchup is advertised on anti-TV with a backward rendition of the anti-Carly Simon hit "Cipation."

Taking Up Ropewalking

 ʼʼʼ

Because Uncle Al has only occasional custody of the aging but ever-sarcastic small dog Lucky, he feels somewhat constrained to keep up the rituals that are part of the warp and woof—well, at least the woof—of Lucky's regular life. Uncle Al thinks some of these rituals are kind of dumb, but he doesn't want to untrain Lucky by not keeping them up.

Thus, for example, when Lucky tires of hanging around Uncle Al's chair while Uncle Al eats, and he eventually finishes off what's in his own dish, he always comes by and makes kind of a pest of himself until he is given a dog treat. That's the deal he has at home: Finish your dinner, get a treat.

Giving Lucky something to eat as a reward for finishing what's in his dish has always seemed like a bad idea to Uncle Al, but he has to acknowledge that despite his misgivings it probably won't cause Lucky to develop an eating disorder when he grows up and moves away from home.

So when Lucky starts to pester, Uncle Al always goes out to the kitchen and checks his bowl. "Did you finish your dinner?" he asks. "What a good boy," the sequence continues. "Do you want a treat?"

Sometimes Lucky just dances around waiting for Uncle Al to fish the yummy nugget of bone meal and soy by-products out of the box, but sometimes at this point Uncle Al finds himself letting Lucky give vent to his curmudgeonly aspect.

"Is 'Did you finish your dinner?' a rhetorical question?"

Lucky once asked, "because you can see my dish is empty. What do you want me to do, file an amended 1099?"

It was during one of Lucky's recent visits that the two grand progressions of Uncle Al's mental life (this state of mind that allows him to voice the independent thoughts of a dog, and the general loss of the rest of his mind) came together like the expertly woven separate narratives of a suspense novel, in which the lives of the politician, the assassin, the detective, the innocent bystander and the fish-cannery union organizer are all developed on separate tracks that meet in a blinding moment seen from many perspectives. (Except that the fish-cannery union organizer, of course, turns out to be a red herring.)

Anyway, Uncle Al got up one morning during that visit from Lucky, got ready to take him for his morning walk, and went to the front door, where he always drapes Lucky's leash over the handle. The leash wasn't there. Uncle Al looked around the floor near the door, where it might have fallen, and it wasn't there, either.

Uncle Al poked under nearby furniture to see whether it had somehow gotten kicked out of sight; it hadn't.

OK, Uncle Al thought, he must have taken it into the kitchen when he came in with Lucky last night. No problem, except that a quick perusal of the kitchen turned up no leash.

By this time, Lucky, who is almost seventeen and, understandably, can be a little lethargic at times, was far from it. In fact, he was so desperate to go out, and to break through what seemed to be Uncle Al's poorly timed decision to wander around the house, that he was practically turning handsprings.

Uncle Al gave up and, knowing that he had a hank of rope outside, took a scissors and managed to cut off a piece to use as a leash. Getting Lucky to hold still while Uncle Al tied the rope to his collar was no small feat, but eventually that got taken care of, and they had a perfectly nice walk.

When he got home after work that night, after a quick glance around the living room failed to reveal the leash, Uncle Al used the rope again, promising himself to undertake a thorough search when he and Lucky got back home.

He began the search with a careful inspection of the only places he might have gone when he and Lucky came in the previous night with Lucky's leash still on—to the kitchen phone, to answer an urgent call probably from a telemarketer, or to the bathroom, to answer an urgent call from Nature. The leash was in neither place.

Given that, Uncle Al reasoned, and given that his unvarying habit is to put the leash on the front door handle, he had to consider the possibility that Lucky himself might have pulled the leash off the door handle and taken it somewhere.

In the almost 15 years Uncle Al has known him, Lucky has never bitten, chewed or taken anything that wasn't placed on the floor for him to bite, chew or take, so it was very unlikely that he had walked off with his leash. But because he had no pattern of such activity, if he had taken the leash there was no way for Uncle Al to guess where he might have gone with it.

Thus, Uncle Al spent an entire evening looking behind, under and between various pieces of furniture, under his bed, in the upstairs bathroom and—gulp—in the basement. If Lucky's goal had been to hide his leash for all time, he could not have chosen a better location than the basement.

Uncle Al looked behind as many boxes, bags and stacks of stuff as he could manage without hours of heavy lifting. (Yes, regular readers, he looked next to his funnels. No, regular readers, he did not look in a safe-deposit box in Milwaukee.)

Uncle Al must acknowledge that, throughout this increasingly frustrating search, as he looked in stupider and stupider places, he was accompanied by Lucky, who kept up a fairly constant and insulting patter:

"It's not behind the wash machine, huh, Al? [He always calls Uncle Al "Al" with icy disdain, as if the word is an insult.] Why don't you unfasten the kitchen drain? I might have dropped it down there."

And "I'm only a dog, Al, but even I can think of more productive ways to spend a whole evening. Licking my feet and staring at the window, for one."

And, most annoying, "Say, Al, why don't you just buy a new leash?"

That would have been a fine solution, except that the leash goes back about as far as Lucky does—it's the only thing that transfers houses with him (Uncle Al has sometimes referred to it as Lucky's "worldly good," which Lucky doesn't appreciate)—and the woman who normally runs the can opener for Lucky probably would be very unhappy to learn that Uncle Al had somehow lost it.

Lucky knew all of that and suggested "just" buying a new leash anyway. Smart aleck!

Next morning, Uncle Al walked Lucky with the rope again, once more looking under and behind everything near the living room door. That evening, when he got home from work, he used the rope again.

But when he and Lucky got back from that walk, Uncle Al noted the particularly high level of clutter that had achieved itself in the living room, and he decided that, to avoid adding to it, he would hang up his coat instead of following his habit of tossing it over what has become "the outerwear chair." So he crossed the four steps to the closet, reached to open the door, and on that door handle saw the leash, in plain view—where he had put it when he had put away a jacket in a similar fit of tidiness the other evening.

"There it is, Lucky!" Uncle Al exclaimed. "There's your leash! It was right here all the time!"

"What a good job, Al!" Lucky smirked. "Do you want a treat?"

Beef or Chicken? Or Beans?

Everyone likes a good laugh, and there's nothing Uncle Al enjoys more than a report by an economist—unless it's a report by several economists.

Thus, Uncle Al was practically on the floor not long ago when a commission of no less than five economists undertook to simultaneously praise and criticize the Consumer Price Index.

The good thing about the CPI, they said, is that the cost of its unchanging "market basket" of 95,000 goods and services indicates how prices change over time.

The bad thing, they said, is that keeping the list of things in that market basket unchanged fails to reflect what consumers really do. For example, the panel's chairman, Stanford University economist Michael Boskin, said: When the price of beef gets too high, consumers don't buy the beef; they switch to chicken, and thus they don't necessarily spend more.

(Economists have this information about consumer behavior secondhand. What economists themselves do if beef goes up is to buy chicken futures.)

If you took into account things like consumers switching from beef to chicken, Boskin said, the CPI would not rise as much. The way the CPI is now constituted, the economists agreed, it overstates how much the real cost of living is going up.

Sound thinking, Uncle Al agrees, and he notes that later,

when the price of chicken gets too high, consumers switch to soup bones, and after that to beans and rice, then to powdered milk, and then to government-surplus cheese.

It gets a little complicated when consumers run out of protein products to switch among, but in any case it's clear that, when you look at it this way, the cost of whatever is in that "beef" category of the "market basket" never goes up!

Similar substitutions can be noted for almost all categories of the price index. Cost of kid's bicycle went up? Substitute repair of bicycle outgrown and abandoned by older kid. Bicycle repair price up? Substitute pogo stick. Pogo stick going up? Tell kid to walk.

The delightful result of all this is that it's possible to demonstrate through multiple successive substitutions that the cost of living has never gone up at all!

Uncle Al loves economics!

Those who know Uncle Al will not be surprised that he was not hugely swayed by the commission's report. (And it's a good thing: Uncle Al being hugely swayed is not pretty.) But he is prepared to agree with the kind of analysis offered in the report when it comes to one consumer product: greeting cards.

Uncle Al has reached the point in his life that he is considering buying a gross of sympathy cards, just to cut down on the number of trips he has to make to the store as everyone around him drops dead, but his bigger gripe is that the price of greeting cards has gone through the roof.

A typical card, no matter how plain, suddenly is $2.50 or $3 or more—way past anything that would seem to resemble its cost. It's a piece of paper with printing on one side, folded in four. Even with the no doubt princely fees paid to the writers, artists, printers, and paper folders involved, how much could that possibly cost?

Maybe the price of paper is a factor in the increase—comic books, magazines and newspapers (in decreasing order of their value to society) are all way up in price. It would be hard to follow the lead of economists in those cases: There's no such thing as switching to a cheaper but otherwise equivalent comic book; dropping a *Vogue* subscription because *Reader's Digest* costs less isn't satisfactory either, and it's difficult to find a less expensive newspaper that carries the same annoying features.

But greeting cards . . .

If you can fold a piece of paper, you can make your own greeting card. We have the technology.

It's hard to find plain envelopes that will hold a 4¼- by 5½-inch item (a folded 8½- by 11-inch sheet), except at a card store, where they won't love selling them to you without the cards they came with. But you can buy a manila envelope that isn't much too large, or you can use a piece of wrapping paper cut and folded—and held together with whatever best fits your personality: glue, Scotch tape, masking tape, duct tape or staples.

Probably, though, it isn't the envelope problem that keeps most folks from making their own greeting cards; it's the greeting. It was worth a buck or so not to have to think of something to say to your cousin Moobel on her birthday or to your rather strange nephew when he graduates from high school.

But when the card costs $3 or $4, Uncle Al observes, it's not all that difficult to come up with your own instead.

Besides saving money, writing your own greeting card allows you to address both the specific occasion and the recipient much more concretely and personally than is possible with a store-bought card. Here are some examples.

- For a newly announced divorce: "I never did like him [or her]."
- For the person downsized out of a 20-year career: "I hope you cleaned out the supply cabinet."
- For a new friend: "Everything is much clearer to me now that I've met your parents."
- For the person who is divorcing your ex-spouse: "I could have told you so."
- For the birthday of an elderly aunt, who is very funny but is fed up with "boy-are-you-old" jokes: "Happy birthday! You've been more fun at 88 than any two of my 44-year old friends. I can't wait to see what you do at 89."
- For the birthday of an economist: "Happy Birthday! I was going to get you some pâté but the price went up, so I bought you half a pound of liverwurst."

The Scent of a Guy

ᕽᕽᕽ

Every once in a while I read or see something that indicates how difficult it is to spend a lot of money.

Let's say you win the lottery, for example, or are signed by the New York Yankees. After you rush out and buy a few mansions and a bunch of expensive but unreliable vehicles, there are only so many suits of armor, antique popcorn machines and silk parkas that you can purchase before you begin to run out of things you want—and run out of places to put the stuff you bought on the off chance you might want it later.

So we're told, anyway.

I am grateful that I have never been forced to face that horrible situation. Recently, however, I came as close as I hope I ever will.

The trouble started, naturally enough, with some bad luck: I was unfortunate this year in that I didn't get sick as often as I expected I would, so unless I came up with some way out of the situation, I was about to forfeit a chunk of money from my health-care flexible-spending account.

The health-care flexible-spending account is a tax dodge that lets you set aside some money for the year's health-care expenses. The good part is that you don't have to pay any income tax on that money. The bad part is that you have to commit at the beginning of the year to how much you're depositing in that account each payday, and if there's any money left unspent on medical matters at the end of the year, you lose it.

I have been depositing $10 a week, and with my bad luck have been so wretchedly healthy that I will have almost $300 left in my account at the end of the year. It can't be spent on anything but health-care stuff, and it must be spent this year or it will be forfeited.

I've reduced the amount I'm going to have withheld next year; with luck I'll be sick enough to spend all of the smaller total. In the meantime, I needed to come up with something medical on which to spend this year's $300 surplus, perhaps a set of dentures or an emergency appendectomy.

The thought is that it would be better to spend the money on something—even if it's something I don't need at all—than to throw it away.

Yes, it is stupid to make me buy something useless with the money instead of, say, letting me give it to charity; this is your federal tax code at work.

An emergency appendectomy was not practical in my case, because I had one many years ago, and doctors seem adamant about limiting these to one per customer. I don't wear dentures, and pulling all my teeth so I'd need dentures would go well past the $300 I wanted to spend.

So I decided early this month that, if my bad luck held and I still had the $300 late this month, I would get a new pair of glasses. There's nothing really wrong with my present bifocals; they're great for reading the computer screen. But they're not good for doing crossword puzzles, and I figured I'd experiment with a different kind of bifocal.

I'll keep this relatively short by omitting the discussion with the optometrist at the mall optical store, in which he told me why he didn't think I'd like what I thought I wanted.

The upshot was that suddenly I had nothing to waste my $300 on.

That's how I came to know something of the bitterness of the lottery winner or the Yankees recruit. The $300 was burning a hole in my pocket, and I was going to be unable to quench that flame.

I explained my dilemma. The doctor understood and had a helpful suggestion: "How about prescription sunglasses?"

Hmm. Never had those. OK.

Out in the optical store, I picked a dark frame for no particular reason, and I was steered to dark gray lenses to match them. OK, too.

I had a while to kill until the glasses would be ready, so I did some other shopping, returning to the optical store through a large department store. In the men's-cologne area, a woman giving out samples started toward me, got a better look, clearly decided I wasn't the cologne type, and moved away.

I had the glasses fitted, caught a look at myself in the mirror on the way out of the optical store, and was startled. I looked cool!

"That's not Uncle Al, the dork," I thought. "That's Tommy Lee Jones!"

It was empowering. As I passed through the same department store, I stared through potential pests left and right. The same cologne woman retreated from me again, but this time I suspected—no, I knew—that it was from respect, not disdain.

Here was a whole new Uncle Al, infinitely self-assured behind those shades: the imperturbable master of his fate.

I wore the glasses to work the next day, and I left them

on in the office even though they made my terminal a little hard to read and they rendered the whole office a little dim. The effect, augmented by black shirt and black pants, was gratifying.

Except for those folks (in the large majority) who assumed that I was wearing the dark glasses because of some age-related eye condition, the most common reaction was one expressed by a manager: "You hadn't struck me as a shades kind of guy."

"I am now, Pilgrim," I responded, deciding that his expression said exactly what I was looking for: "Ooh. I guess I'd better back away a little from this guy."

I don't really understand why concealing my pupils transforms me from pleasant schnook to urban man of iron, but clearly it does.

I have no doubt that what people are whispering to each other as I pass is, "I'd never recognized Al's calm, masterful grace." (I know that it is not what I seem to hear over the age-related ringing in my ears: "I'd never recognized that Al's a dumb basket case.")

And I walk a little taller as a result.

When you see me coming, better step aside: A lot of men didn't, and a lot of men got bumped into because it's a little hard to see them.

Best $300 I ever wasted.

Heads Up!

You might have missed the following news, since it came in the middle of last year's nonexistent Christmas shopping frenzy, and you might have been distracted by endless phone calls from economic analysts wanting to know why you weren't out buying something.

But now that Christmas and Valentine's Day are out of the way, as are Presidents' Day, Ramadan, and Hanukkah, we can turn our attention completely to the matter of the malfunctioning Chinese spy satellite that scientists expect to fall to earth by the beginning of April.

Now, your normal malfunctioning satellite burns up quite nicely when it reenters the atmosphere, and only something like the charred scraps of English muffin that you can't ever get out of the toaster survive to rain down onto puzzled soccer fans in Argentina.

However, this particular satellite, which is heavily shielded and weighs about two tons, was designed to parachute to earth intact and be picked up by the Chinese army.

Unfortunately for the folks who wanted to look at the satellite's spy photographs (I believe there's a nice one of me, buying Canadian candy in Acapulco), it began to function erratically ten days after it was launched in October 1993. It went into a decaying orbit, with a low point that, at the time of the December news report, was down to a hundred miles.

The best bet among rocket scientists is that the satellite,

known as an FSW-1, will come down somewhere at sea and will sink like a stone, but they are offering two other scenarios.

First is that the satellite somehow will figure out on its way down that it's supposed to deploy its parachute (these guys are rocket scientists, but they're not exactly rocket scientists) and will then float serenely down to earth—into Tivoli Gardens in Copenhagen, perhaps, or the parking lot of a Burger King in East Moline, Illinois, or maybe partway through the skylight of a council house in suburban London.

The second possibility seems more likely than that. It's surely more interesting:

The FSW-1's parachute won't deploy, but it won't come down at sea, and it will survive the descent because it is so heavily shielded. In other words, a white-hot hunk of metal that weighs something like a couple of Honda Civics will come barreling out of the sky at maybe 20,000 feet a minute, giving somebody on the ground a chance to look up and say "Holy Toledo! I think that's the FS . . ."

Besides reconnaissance systems and exposed film, the satellite also contains a diamond-studded medallion of Mao Zedong. Really.

So if the satellite doesn't get smashed up too badly when it demolishes your car or whatever, we can expect the Chinese army to come by to pick up their film (there are 1.2 billion people in China, so they'll probably want double prints), and a contingent of professional dingus hunters left over from the St. Paul Winter Carnival will doubtless swarm over the crash site searching for the medallion.

European and U.S. analysts cited in *Aviation Week & Space Technology* magazine predicted a reentry in February or March. But Major Don Planalp, a spokesman for the U.S. Space Command in Colorado Springs, Colorado, told the *New York Times* that 11 sensors were tracking the satellite closely and that its reentry date was estimated to be April 1.

(Planalp is not to be confused with Robert Abplanalp, buddy of President Nixon and inventor of the aerosol can— nor with Nixon's other friend, Florida banker Bebe Rebozo, nor with imaginary Florida clown Bozo Rebebe.)

Not mentioned in the *New York Times* report was the possibility that the crash would occur on April 1, as Planalp predicted, and that last-minute warnings would be taken for April Fool pranks:

"Is your house on Minnehaha Avenue? Well, look out because there's a two-ton Chinese satellite falling on it."

"Yeah, sure. Ha, ha, ha."

"No, really."

"Yeah, and then I bet there's a won-ton Chinese satellite falling on it. Ha, ha."

"No, reall . . . Oh-oh. Eeewww. Sorry."

A New Dog's Blanket Endorsement

ᴖᴖᴖ

A few field notes on recent events in the life of Uncle Al, to permit the telling of a tiny tale and the propounding of an important new Rule for Living:

As readers of the Travel section might already know, Travel editor Catherine Watson's swell little dog, Lucky, who roomed with Uncle Al whenever Watson was on the road, died last September.

Lucky had stuck around for both of us as long as he could— he was 17½—and although Uncle Al wasn't actually related to him, so to speak, he really missed him. And so—to make what could be a much longer but not very interesting column at least a shorter but not very interesting column—a month or so ago he went to a shelter and got another dog. So, soon after, did Watson. (It's not a surprise to either her or Uncle Al that if Lucky had worn shoes, it would take two dogs to fill them.)

Uncle Al's dog, Fuzzy, is impressively cuddly for a fairly large dog. His idea of a good time is somebody petting him—with both hands. His idea of an even better time is two people petting him—with four hands. If any of those hands is removed, he whimpers until it is returned.

So far, unlike Lucky, Fuzzy hasn't seemed to want to say sarcastic things about Uncle Al.

On another front (but trust Uncle Al, all this will come together soon): Uncle Al's current vehicle is the same now-10-year-old truck whose door he wrecked a couple of years ago when he let the truck roll out of the garage with that door open.

That's been his only real problem with the truck—until the windshield washer quit a few weeks ago. There wasn't anything wrong with the windshield washer, but one cold day the windshield-washer-button part of the far-too-many-functions stick on the steering column broke off.

Replacing the whole far-too-many-functions stick would create a far-too-many-dollars dent in Uncle Al's wallet, so he wired a doorbell button to run the windshield washer, and he plans to spend many happy hours this summer attempting to glue the broken part back onto the far-too-many-functions stick (without gluing all the other far-too-many functions together).

Uncle Al really had no reason to bring that up except to note that it caused him (and others at the lunch table whom he dragged into the discussion) to attempt without much success to recall what any of them did to keep their windshields clear of spattered winter road muck before there were windshield washers.

About all anyone came up with was that people stopped often to clear their windshields with snow. Uncle Al opined that he should perhaps ask an old person, producing a great deal of unnecessary mirth from his lunch cronies, all along the lines of "And how much older than you would 'an old person' be?"

The third (and last) development of note (hang on, we're almost to what Uncle Al continues to believe will be the point) is that he recently joined the last century by acquiring a cell phone. He did it not so he could chat with his many admirers while driving his truck, shopping for groceries or waiting out the duller parts of major motion pictures, but mostly in case other portions of his truck broke off while he was on the road.

OK. Here (finally) is the scene: On Christmas morning, with temperatures somewhat below zero, Uncle Al and Fuzzy had been out visiting, and were heading home in the truck, when a sudden multiple thump sounded from up front. One glance under the hood confirmed that the belt that runs everything, including the water pump, was in shreds.

The engine would fry if Uncle Al tried to get home without that belt—unless, he realized much later, he did so in short jumps, letting the engine cool off in between. Good thinking, or it would have been had he thought of it then. But he didn't think of it then, probably partly because the situation allowed him to use his snazzy new phone instead of figuring out how to get home.

He called a roadside emergency service and was told that although everything in town was closed for Christmas, a tow truck would be by in about 45 minutes to take his truck somewhere to be repaired the next day.

That good news didn't keep the inside of the truck from getting cold in almost no time. That's when Uncle Al remembered the winter emergency pack he had put together six or seven years before, and he hauled it out from behind the seat. It contained, among other things, a blanket, a pack of chocolate-covered granola bars and a large chocolate bar.

The blanket was great. Uncle Al covered Fuzzy and himself with it and found that it provided a surprising amount of relief, partly because Fuzzy, being a dog, runs warmer than Uncle Al does—and because, being Fuzzy, he sqwudged himself onto Uncle Al's lap under the blanket so he could be petted.

But the chocolate—both the chocolate bar and the granola bars—had suffered from being exposed to six or seven cycles of summer melting and winter freezing. The chocolate bar was powder, and the coating on the granola bars became powder when Uncle Al bit into one. He ate it anyway, but with great sadness for what might have been.

Eventually the tow truck came, dropped Uncle Al's truck at a closed repair place and took him and Fuzzy home in time for Uncle Al to thaw out his shoes and get a ride so he and Fuzzy could join friends for dinner. A tiny story, with a happy ending.

And the promised important new Rule for Living:

Just as you should change the batteries in your watch and your smoke detector once a year (one suggestion is to do it every April, when you set your clocks ahead for daylight saving time), Uncle Al recommends that you stock your winter survival kit with your favorite candy bars. Then once a year (perhaps on your birthday) you should replace them with new ones—and eat all of the old ones, while they're still yummy.

It's not often that life presents you with a situation in which not only there's a whole bunch of candy that can be eaten, but it's actually a good idea to eat it. Uncle Al urges you to seize that opportunity.

It's one thing to freeze to death, after all; it's quite another to freeze to death while staring at a pile of dust that used to be a candy bar.

Cellar Beware

ⲧⲧⲧ

Uncle Al is at once proud and chagrined to report that his latest home-maintenance project set a new all-time record high (as we say in the Department of Repetitive Redundancy) in number of trips to the hardware store.

Uncle Al can't say exactly how many such trips were involved because he lost count, but he is sure that the number was at least 12—the whole thing took up a large part of the last four days of his vacation. (Uncle Al knows how to have a good time.)

In any case, he is certain that he easily shattered his previous mark of eight, set several years ago in the regrettable affair of the indisposed disposal.

It was that project that convinced him that the Rule of Three Trips holds only for projects that a normal person would tackle on a weekend. Larger enterprises might have a three-trip minimum, but there is no theoretical maximum.

The significance of Uncle Al's latest undertaking is not only that it set a new benchmark, which even he will find it difficult to surpass, but also that on one of its earliest hardware store visits he encountered the first independent acknowledgment of the multiple-trip syndrome.

To render the whole grueling story in full detail—although it would surely be hilarious to those who delight in others' misery—would try the patience of decent folks, so Uncle Al will summarize. But to provide even the most minimal comprehensibility (as ever, Uncle Al's goal is the most minimal comprehensibility), he must describe the problem he set out to repair.

When Uncle Al bought his house about 10 years ago, he was delighted to note that its basement wasn't very basementy. Even the laundry room was clean and airy, and it included a little bathroom-type sink and cabinet. The room was so delightful that there wasn't even one of those ugly laundry tubs.

Although Uncle Al didn't plan to while away many happy hours in the laundry room, he found its cheerful aspect appealing, and he didn't notice until much later that there also seemed to be no floor drain.

And although it is now apparent to him that he should have found both of those omissions noteworthy (and that he should have wondered "So where is the discharge hose from the washer, which should be hooked onto the side of the missing ugly laundry tub?"), he didn't (and he didn't).

Then one day last month there was a puddle on the laundry room floor.

It now appears that some previous inmate had removed the laundry tub, replaced it with the bathroom-type sink and cabinet, neatly hiding the washer's discharge hose behind the cabinet and connecting it directly to the sink's drain pipe with duct tape.

One of the several reasons that duct-taping the laundry hose into a hidden drain pipe has not achieved wide popularity among owners of the nation's basements is that the wash water contains a fair amount of lint and other laundry squeezings, which if you can see the end of the discharge hose you can trap with a sock or something instead of sending it all straight to wherever in the drain looks like a good place to clog.

A many-year accumulation of such stuff, Uncle Al assumes, is what finally caused the puddle on his floor, which led him to discover, as he disassembled the bathroom-type cabinet so he could replace it with an ugly laundry tub, that the missing floor drain, fully clogged, was underneath the (waterlogged) bottom of the $%#&# cabinet.

To be fair (although to whom this is fair Uncle Al is not at all sure), at least three of his 12 or so hardware store trips didn't involve buying plumbing supplies (or slightly different replacements for the plumbing supplies bought on the previous trip), but were devoted instead to the purchase of better (or different, or worse) blades for the reciprocating saw with which Uncle Al whiled away an afternoon endlessly cutting out a section of the $%#&# cast-iron drain pipe from the sink.

(This was so he could install an opening into which, in the event of later clogs, an older, wiser Uncle Al might insert a hand-cranked clog remover.)

The pipe was so close to a corner of the wall that the end of the $%#&# reciprocating blade kept hitting the wall while it reciprocated. This typically bent the blade badly, and after Uncle Al unbent the blade and tried to use it, it would then break.

(Before all of that, of course, Uncle Al had spent about an hour trying to remember where he had put his $%#&# reciprocating saw.)

But it was on a trip earlier in the project (to buy the ugly laundry tub) that Uncle Al encountered the aforementioned groundbreaking independent acknowledgment of this entire multi-trip syndrome.

Because for a moment it seemed to Uncle Al that the size of pipe he was replacing fell between two standard sizes, he asked a helpful hardware guy if there was a standard size between those two. The hardware guy said there wasn't, and Uncle Al turned back to the shelves in thought.

"Anything I can help you with?" the hardware guy asked.

"No," said Uncle Al, deep in puzzled introspection.

"OK," said the hardware guy, clearly detecting a case of the Rule of At Least Three Trips in process. "See you in a couple hours."

"Actually," said Uncle Al a few moments later, recovering his aplomb (or in this case, his aplumb), "it's probably going to be longer than that; I have to unfasten some old pipe first." This was before the saw entered the picture: At this stage, Uncle Al was hoping (against hope) to merely unscrew bits of the old plumbing and insert new bits to meet his needs.

With that in mind, he asked the hardware guy if he had a recommendation for something to loosen rusted cast-iron pipe joints. He expected to be directed to a product, such as WD-40 or Liquid Wrench.

"Anger," said the hardware guy. "And profanity."

Much anger and profanity later, when Uncle Al finished replacing the cabinet and sink with the newly plumbed ugly tub—a project he had felt (more or less correctly) was within his area of competence (but that in fact turned out to be rather more less than more)—he called a professional to clear out the newly discovered clogged floor drain.

Uncle Al might be stupidly fixated on doing things himself, but even he has limits.

Pledge Week for Humor

ᕯᕯᕯ

Coming up in just a little bit, another of those hilarious, wide-ranging humor columns you usually find in this spot. But right now it's time to be serious for just a moment.

As a regular or occasional reader of this humor service, you are probably aware that it isn't free. Somebody has to pay for it. Subscription or newsstand payments for the newspaper don't even begin to cover the costs of the wide-ranging humor you're accustomed to finding right here. Advertiser dollars help, of course, as do grants from organizations like The Corporation for Humor in Newspapers and the Marcel Marceau/Harpo Marx Foundation for Silent Communication. But they don't pay it all either.

And that's where you come in.

Yes, it's Readership Week at the *Star Tribune,* the time when we ask you to renew your sponsorship of this fine wide-ranging humor column.

Imagine for a moment what your life would be like without it.

There would be nothing to offer that range of thought-provoking advice and self-absorbed commentary that you have come to expect.

And it's your contribution that helps make all this possible. Here's corporate chief accountant Nelson Fung to help explain.

"Thanks, Al. First let me say how much I look forward

to all these fund drives because it gives me a chance to get to really know all you readers out there. Of course you don't say anything back, but . . . And I am a little nervous because the rest of the year I never write all that much. But what I want to say is that the fact that you are able to read this column doesn't mean we can afford to keep on producing it. We could go broke. We're not that far from it. We certainly don't pay Al all that much, do we, Al, ha, ha?"

No, you don't, Nelson. Ha, ha.

"Now that's the kind of wide-ranging humor you find here every week. And if you like that kind of humor, if you want to keep it coming, if you don't want to see that wide-ranging humor cut back so it doesn't range very wide at all and gets kind of inbred and sickly and pasty-complexioned and makes you want to leave the room and get a suntan, we want you to become a sponsor of this feature service. Or renew your sponsorship. Or maybe just toss us an extra grand or two, what the heck, ha, ha."

Yes. Ha, ha. Thank you very much, Nelson Fung, corporate chief accountant. In just a minute we'll be getting back to those wide-ranging, thought-provoking features you're accustomed to seeing here. But first let's meet Mary Gribbnitz, one of our telephone-answering volunteers. Mary?

"Thanks, Al. We want to make sure folks know how to vote with their fingers, so to speak, by dialing the phone and pledging a few hundred dollars—or a few thousand dollars—to help support this feature service. All this week, of course, your pledge will be matched by the Jennifer and Nathan Stoopmacher Sedentary Arts Fund. And if you dial right now, your pledge is also being matched by the Leonard Garment Foundation for Foundation Garments. So that means your dollar is being tripled. Or is it being quadrupled? I'm not sure, actually. Let's just say that this is a way to make your one dollar do the work of two. *There's* a phone ringing now!"

Yes. This is a very exciting time. And we need you to help by doing your part to support this feature service. Here to help us celebrate all this excitement is assistant publisher Marvin Bilgepump.

"Thank you, Al. This is a very exciting time. And we need you to help by doing your part to support this feature service. That is, we need your help to support this wide-ranging and thought-provoking service. So dig out a credit card and give us a call. Or stop by and call Al down to the lobby and slip him fifty bucks. It all helps. If we're going to win the Concrete Foundation matching grant that will allow us to stay in business, instead of firing Al and going to a light-rock format, we need your pledge right now. Call us at 555-9999. Or, if you're calling from where you can't read this, call us toll-free at 1-800-555-9999. But do it now, before we have to start using up our regular wide-ranging material."

Thank you, Marvin.

"Thank you, Al. And don't forget, when you call, to inquire about attending the Al Sicherman Loyalty Days siding-removal party. Tickets are still available."

Thanks again, Marvin. And if you call right now, and contribute just $10 a month for the rest of your life, you're eligible for our best thank-you gift: a detailed schedule of all our fund-raising activities. So this could be the last time you'll have to encounter Nelson, Marvin and Mary. That's worth a lot more than $10, isn't it, Nelson, ha, ha?

"Shut up, Al, ha, ha."

Running Up Your Life Expectancy

The other day Uncle Al stumbled across one of those fill-in-the-blank online surveys, in which you provide information about your genetics and lifestyle and weight and age and hairdo and whatever. It then poots out how long you might be expected to live.

Thinking about how to slant his answers (yes, Uncle Al cheats on self-help quizzes), Uncle Al knows that his preference for not exercising—particularly for not dragging himself around his neighborhood in running shorts at 6 a.m., looking like death—has a negative impact on his probable lifespan. And he knows that other aspects of his lifestyle, especially his intake of chocolate, egg yolks, cream and butter, don't help much, either.

But while he's very unlikely to start alarming dogs and motorists by staggering around the block every morning, he's *certainly* not giving up chocolate eclairs. So he decided to fill out the questionnaire with complete honesty once, and then go back and change his answers to questions about how much he exercises, and maybe some other things, in order to see how much difference they would make. Diet changes were not going to be on the table.

With completely honest answers, the calculator at http://www.livingto100.com reported that Uncle Al might expect to live to age 83.4. After he threw in a 20-minute daily jog, the calculator came back with a life expectancy of 86.2 years: If Uncle Al ran 20 minutes a day, he'd gain 2.8 years!

So, having learned that changes he might make could have significant bearing on the matter, Uncle Al went back through the quiz, looking for changes that would be as effective as exercise but less painful.

Uncle Al doesn't drink to speak of, but moderate alcohol consumption is associated with lower risk of heart disease, so he changed his answer to that question and picked up six-tenths of a year, to 84.

Uncle Al learned, from notes that accompany the results, that living near enough to relatives to be able to drop in on them is healthful, as it provides coping help and lowers stress. He doesn't live near relatives, so he had answered "no" to that question; when he made it "yes" (along with taking up drinking), his life expectancy rose to 85.8 years.

That's just 146 days less than the 86.2 years he'd get by running 20 minutes a day!

Uncle Al fired up his pencil and found that slogging 20 minutes a day for a year takes 121 hours—5.07 entire days.

In the 24.2 years Uncle Al has before he would be 86.2, the 5.07 days a year he'd have to run to live that long would total 123 days of running: He'd have to run 123 days in order to live 146 days more than if he just started drinking and dropping in on relatives and didn't run.

Running would give him a net gain of only 23 days! They would have to be 23 pretty good days.

Some time when he has little else to occupy his giant brain, Uncle Al might make a list of what deeply satisfying things he'd do with 23 extra days at age 86. Stay tuned.

Uncle Al must admit that he glossed over a significant difficulty in the matter of dropping in on relatives instead of running: His only blood relatives are his son in New York and a niece and a couple of nephews in Milwaukee, so it would be no small matter to arrange to live in drop-by distance of any of them and still stay within driving distance of people he does drop in on, in Minneapolis.

He decided to see if any other life expectancy calculators offered further insights.

The first one he pulled up, offered by BBCi, the Internet presence of the British Broadcasting Corporation, was very similar to the one at www.livingto100.com.

It had no entry for not drinking at all, but except for that, Uncle Al filled it out exactly as he had the other one, and he was surprised to find he had a life expectancy of 86.4 years—and, if he lived near relatives, 88.2!

So a great idea would be to move to England! On the other hand, there Uncle Al would be, living three years longer than his original 83.4 but not knowing a soul to drop in on. Uncle Al's son Dave would never leave New York, but maybe he could persuade his niece to move from Milwaukee to England, so he could live to 88.2.

The next life expectancy calculator he looked at, at a Web site called Fastfa.com, a financial analysis firm, had quite a different set of questions, resulting in quite a different result: 77.7 years. That wasn't great news, but Uncle Al found the way it was presented to be even more stressful:

"Your life expectancy is: 77.7 years. That means you have 15.7 years to get your finances in order. Click here to learn about our Fastfa Financial Analysis programs and spend your final 15.7 years free of financial worries."

But for downright spookiness, nothing tops the Early Warning Life Expectancy calculator at http://home.worldonline.dk/eskemj/, a Danish site. It asks only birth date and time, gender and country, so it isn't a personal forecast; ostensibly it provides the average life expectancy for someone of that age. But again the presentation left something to be desired, and it was compounded by a glitch.

The answer is posted as "You can expect to live another . . ." above a digital countdown clock showing how many years, days, hours, minutes and seconds one has left. Uncle Al advises: Avoid this site if you don't live near relatives.

When Uncle Al did it, the posted answer was three seconds!

When he reflexively hit the button again (very hard, and in far less than three seconds), the readout changed to 20 minutes, three seconds. Uncle Al quit then, as that at least gave him enough time to hop in his car, drive to a bakery and buy a chocolate eclair.

Fuzzy Has Cake and Eats It Too

ʅʅʅ

For two compelling reasons, this seems to Uncle Al to be a good time to update folks on the unfolding saga of his relatively new dog, Fuzzy.

For one thing, Fuzzy (that's the name he came with from the shelter, and because it was his only possession—and because he *is* fuzzy—Uncle Al felt he should keep it) has barely been mentioned lately, and there have been several notable developments.

And—even more compelling—Uncle Al's brilliant idea for today's column, which he scribbled on one of the many pieces of paper he keeps in little piles around his house, seems unaccountably to have disappeared (and, of course, all Uncle Al can remember about it is that it was brilliant).

So. Fuzzy, who is swell, needs to be petted constantly. With both hands when possible. Otherwise he whimpers and bonks the offending hand with his head, making it very hard for that hand to, for example, hold the newspaper.

(Uncle Al is delighted to have this new excuse for why he seems to be out of the loop on so many current events. "Fuzzy didn't let me read the paper at all yesterday," he is now able to explain. "I'm only keeping my subscription because those yellow plastic bags are so good for picking up dog poop.")

To fully comprehend the following tale, it is necessary to understand how Fuzzy is arranged. With all four feet on the floor, he is a smallish dog, about Lucky's height—his back is maybe 15 inches off the ground. But in fact he is bigger than Lucky was—he just has unusually short legs.

Looked at another way, Fuzzy is about Lucky's size except there's an extra half a dog tacked on the rear.

Looked at still another way (Uncle Al likes looking at things other ways, but this should be the last of this series), Uncle Al followed the advice of an old song and got a long little doggie.

The result of Fuzzy being 1½ dogs long is that on his hind legs he is lots taller than Lucky was—enabling him to reach lots of places that Lucky couldn't. Further, whereas Lucky was a gent, unwilling to eat anything that wasn't given to him, Fuzzy's unwillingness to eat stuff is limited to stuff he can't reach.

Fuzzy has never done any such self-service dining while Uncle Al was around, but on several early occasions Uncle Al came home to find, say, what had been a bag of doughnuts on the kitchen counter transformed into a bag of no doughnuts on the kitchen floor.

It was clear that Fuzzy knew that this was not exemplary behavior. If Fuzzy ran to the end of the sofa farthest from the door when Uncle Al came home in the evening, Uncle Al came to understand that he should look around to find what Fuzzy had eaten during the day, and should make disapproving noises.

If Uncle Al didn't look around before trying to take Fuzzy on his walk (or didn't discover what Fuzzy had eaten—or didn't at least pretend to find it), Fuzzy jumped up and down until he did.

The only choices seemed to be to somehow train Fuzzy

not to find and eat things when he was alone, or to lock Fuzzy up when he was alone.

Uncle Al decided both of those choices would be too hard (on Uncle Al), so he built shelves above the kitchen table for stuff that had been on the table and the counter, moving everything out of Fuzzy's reach.

That worked fine for about two days, until he left a bag full of newspapers for recycling on the kitchen floor near the table. Fuzzy knocked the bag over, giving him enough height to climb onto the table and transform what had been a bag of dog treats on one of the new shelves into a bag of no dog treats on the table.

The next step, removing from the kitchen floor everything Fuzzy could stand on, worked until Fuzzy figured out that he could nudge a kitchen chair far enough from the table to allow him to get onto it, thence to the table, the shelves, and the bags of doughnuts and dog treats.

Uncle Al had been unable to gauge how quickly and how adaptably Fuzzy approached the challenges that Uncle Al posed for him until one day when he was baking a cake as part of his Taste section duties. (Uncle Al was baking, not Fuzzy; Fuzzy doesn't work outside the home.) Uncle Al had, of course, neglected to buy one of the frosting ingredients, so he had to run to the store.

The dining room table had shown itself Fuzzy-proof before (the carpet there made the chairs un-nudgeable), so Uncle Al put the cake in the middle of the table and started to leave, when he had a thought: To ensure that Fuzzy couldn't get onto the table from a chair, he pulled all the chairs away from the table, leaving them along the walls instead.

In the few minutes that Uncle Al was gone, Fuzzy analyzed the situation, got onto a chair, formed himself into a bridge to the table and extensively sampled each layer.

The kitchen was the real problem, though, and a couple of weeks ago Uncle Al took the last possible step: He installed a kitchen door, and he closes it when he leaves. Not only has this halted Fuzzy's unapproved interactions with the food supply, Fuzzy hasn't even scratched the door.

And he seems happy. Now he hides when Uncle Al comes home only if he has made a mess of some of Uncle Al's piles of paper, which are messy to start with, so Uncle Al really doesn't mind.

Unless . . . Has Fuzzy, locked away from his daytime supply of snacks, found solace in sampling Uncle Al's little piles of paper, searching for pieces with flavorful food stains? Could that be what happened to Uncle Al's brilliant idea for today's column?

If so, it might be the first newspaper column in history to completely skip the steps of writing, editing and printing, and go directly into one of those yellow plastic bags.

Rhyme Time Not Sublime

ᕽᕽᕽ

One Sunday several months ago I was reading the comics when I was struck, not by a perhaps-well-deserved blunt object but by a remarkable advertisement. The National Library of Poetry, it said, was having a poetry contest, with $24,000 in prizes to be awarded over the coming year.

"Many submitted poems," it said, "will also be considered for inclusion in one of The National Library of Poetry's forthcoming hardbound anthologies."

Having been taken to the Wisconsin State Fair numerous times by a father whose favorite life-study was guys selling ballpoint pens and cabbage slicers, I learned early in life to look at least twice at every offer. I thought this one sounded not quite straight.

For one thing, I have never heard of "The National Library of Poetry."

I thought I smelled vanity publishing. That's the deal in which you wind up paying, instead of getting paid, to get your book or poetry or sheet music published.

I looked up the Maryland mailing address that was in the ad. The reverse directory showed 16 firms at that address—a contractor, a lighting firm, a software outfit. . . . Not a single poetry library in the bunch. There was (no surprise) a printing firm. Thanks, Dad.

To see just how low in the vanity publishing industry this deal was, I submitted a fully terrible poem under the fictitious name Alben Slimovitz. This was not because I thought The National Library of Poetry would recognize Al Sicherman as the name of a crusading reporter. It allowed me to submit a second—only slightly better—poem under my own name. More about that later.

Editor's note: *Al Sicherman has suddenly taken leave of his senses. The remainder of today's column is being written by his alter ego, Alben Slimovitz, sometime poet, cliché champion and holder of the Melman Prize for Bicycle Safety.*

Hello, everyone out there in newspaperland! I'm tickled pink to be able to pass along this stirring tale.

I submitted for the pleasure of the judges at The National Library of Poetry one of my absolutely top-of-the-heap poems, the tried-and-true "Rain," an early work in the Alben Slimovitz two-poem Weather Cycle.

Now, far be it from me to lay it on thick or play a lot of chin music about how great a poem "Rain" is. You can judge its deliciously lyrical nature for yourself:

I do like to hear the rain
The rain does not give me any pain.
When raining stops the sun comes out
That's the best time to stand up and shout.

In the rainy day is fog and blizzard
That makes a man look old and grizzled.
Never more to see the sky.
That's much worse than you and I.

Puddles splash and splash and splash some more.
And I can see them if I look through my front door.
Oh, how I wish I could get wet
Because I'd run and jump in those puddles, you bet!

*The National Library of Poetry was absolutely agog over my
poem! I received a letter from them saying that the Selection
Committee had certified my poem as a semifinalist in the 1995
North American Open Poetry Contest. "And Alben," it went
on, "in view of your talent, we also wish to publish your poem
in our forthcoming anthology,* The Voice Within.*"*

*It galls me to admit it, but that sniveling journalist,
Al Sicherman, received an identical letter about his stupid
poem about a leaky car radiator. (Oh, how many torments
visit the soul of the true artist!)*

*Back to my poetic triumph: The letter said I could buy a
copy of* The Voice Within *for the special pre-publication
price of $49.95 (and extra copies for $35 each). I purchased
one copy, and I paid another $20 to secure a place in the
volume for my biography. Here's just a part of it:*

Alben Slimovitz. Born Kealakekua, Hawaii; parents Enrico and Kim Slimovitz; married to Desiree
Slimovitz; children Caramel, Iodine and Bob. Member
American Institute of Electrical Engineers and Association of Philippine Coconut Desiccators. Honors
include Melman Prize for Bicycle Safety; Good Posture
Award—ninth grade, King Kamehameha Jr. High . . .
Statement of philosophy: "If you aren't part of the
solution, you are part of the precipitate."

*After time passed, The National Library of Poetry sent me
two more offers: a commemorative plaque on which a copy
of my poem is mounted, for $38, and a reading of the poem
on an audiocassette ($39).*

*Much as my heart leaped at the thought of a plaque
carrying my poem, I am aware that the word "plaque" often
gets confused with "plague," and I didn't want the teeming
masses thinking there was a plague carrying my poem. So
with great reluctance I passed up the plaque, but I couldn't
bring myself to forgo the pleasure of hearing a professional
reader give voice to my poem.*

*Not just everyone got that offer, incidentally. The letter
made that clear: "As our Editors read through the poems
we receive for our contests, they personally select a few
poems that they believe would have a wonderfully expressive quality if read by a professional reader"—and it went
on to say that I was one of "those few poets to whom this
applied."*

*Although it's hard to believe, the poem that Al Sicher-
man submitted under his own name also was judged to be
one of those few that would be wonderfully expressive if
read aloud by a professional reader.*

What are the odds of that?

*Both Al and I submitted forms authorizing publication
of our poems, but only I proceeded to make a number of
purchases. Al, that cheapskate, purchased nothing at all.
The National Library of Poetry had assured each of us, in
its earliest communication, that our poems were selected for
publication—and as contest semifinalists—"solely on the
basis of merit. You are under no obligation whatsoever to*

submit any entry fee, any subsidy payment, or to make any purchase of any kind."

And now The Voice Within *has arrived on my doorstep! My poem is on page 131, if you want to check your copy. The poem by Al, that hack, doesn't appear at all.*

Editor's note: *Al Sicherman couldn't take it anymore and has returned to complete his column.*

I wasn't surprised that my poem wasn't there; I didn't buy anything. (Thanks again for the lesson, Dad.)

I admit that *The Voice Within* is a big, nice-looking book. But inside are a stupefying 4,600 poems—plus 91 pages of biographies and a discussion of the winning poem. (The amount it won isn't clear, but I believe it was $1,000.)

Since each printed poem represents the purchase of at least one book, and there are about 1,500 $20 biographies too, to say nothing of tapes, plaques, etc., this represents a gross of at least $250,000.

Now, I'm no poet; I don't even play one on TV. I don't know what distinguishes a great poem from a good poem—or even a fair poem—but I am confident in saying that among the good and maybe great poems in *The Voice Within* are many that should have stayed within.

Some are so bad that I wonder whether they are the work of other newspaper columnists somewhere testing how low The National Library of Poetry will stoop to get $49.95.

The National Library of Poetry, apparently noting that I've never sent them a nickel, has stopped writing to me. But shortly before the book arrived, moneybags Alben got another letter, saying that the library, having reviewed thousands of submitted poems as well as poetry in other anthologies, had decided to publish "a collection of new poems written by the Best Poets we have encountered.

"I am pleased to tell you, Alben, that you have been selected to appear in this special edition . . . *The Best Poems of the '90s*. . . . Only 2 percent of the individuals whose poetry we have examined were selected to be part of this distinguished group of Outstanding Poets . . . The poem which you will submit for this edition has been accepted for publication sight unseen on the basis of your previous poetic accomplishments. We believe you to be one of the most talented poets we have encountered. . . ."

To see how far this would go, I submitted another Alben poem, about snow. If anything, it was worse than the first. I got an invitation to buy *Best Poems of the '90s,* a plaque and an audiotape.

"A plaque on this whole thing," I thought. "I know how the rest of this goes." But I had underestimated The National Library of Poetry.

The heck with $49.95 books; the next thing Alben got was an invitation to become a Distinguished Member of the International Society of Poets, headquartered, oddly enough, at the same address in Maryland as The National Library of Poetry. That's only $125—plus shipping and handling.

And better still, Alben was invited to attend The International Society of Poets Gala Poetry Symposium and Convention in Washington, D.C., for $495, including several meals (but not hotel room or transportation). Among the attractions listed were entertainment by the Smothers Brothers, Florence

Henderson and The Marvelettes and a seminar appearance by Senator Eugene McCarthy!

The *Star Tribune* has declined my offer to don my beret and black sweater and head for this confab in Washington. That's too bad: Alben was really looking forward to getting McCarthy's reaction to his poem about the 1968 Democratic convention. Here's its opening couplet:

The mayor of Chicago
Did not look very much like Dr. Zhivago.

Three Degrees of Cockeyed

ʻʻʻ

It is with some discomfort that Uncle Al returns to the matter of his kitchen door.

Uncle Al recently referred to it in the context of preventing Fuzzy, his quite elastic chow hound, from eating everything in the kitchen regardless of how far off the floor it was stored. In that exposition, Uncle Al dismissed the affair with the phrase "installed a kitchen door," implying—at least to readers unfamiliar with his methods—that he did it in an hour, with only one trip to the hardware store.

Uncle Al is ashamed for having given that impression, partly because his lack of candor was so obvious that most people who know his work saw through it immediately, and several demanded to know just how badly it had gone.

If he is ever to hold his head up in public (he would say "again," but he never has held his head very high), he feels he must offer a full, frank and candid outline of the process. Only then will he have closure. On the door.

Interestingly (or not), every doorway in Uncle Al's house contains either a door or the ill-disguised spots where hinges and a strike plate once were fastened but from which the door was removed in somebody's long-ago fit of updating. Every doorway, that is, except the one into the kitchen, where Uncle Al found that he needed a door.

Although every project he tackles involves many false starts or false endings and many trips to the hardware store, Uncle Al always begins with a sense that careful planning can eliminate most or all of the situations best characterized by the word "oops."

Thus, and particularly because buying a big, heavy (and not very cheap) door was something he wouldn't want to do a second time because he loused up the first one, Uncle Al thought and thought before he made his first move.

He noted, for example, that the door opening was more than an inch shorter than standard height, and also that the door would need to be a bit shorter than that so it could be opened over the hall carpet. And from a very long (and very unpleasant) day of sawing a door several years ago, he knew that it would be good if somebody else did it.

Thus, having measured the opening and marked where the hinges would go, he had two inches sawed off the door at the store where he bought it. And, having thought ahead, he bought the hinges and the lockset on the same visit; he felt very smug about the whole thing.

He should have known.

It wasn't nearly as bad as it could have been: The door wasn't too short. Or not exactly, anyway.

He had assumed that the doorway in his 80-year-old house consisted of four right angles. Of course, it didn't.

He chiseled hinge positions into both the door and the doorway, fastened the door, and swung it into the closed position. The bottom didn't drag badly on the carpet, and there was a small, uniform space between the latch edge of the door and the matching side of the door frame. But the top of the door frame rose almost an inch between the hinge side and the latch side, leaving a large wedge-shaped opening over the door.

It could have been worse—the doorway could have slanted

down, keeping the door from closing. Still, another hardware run was needed.

Believing that the presence of the gap was what would be noticed, not how it was filled if he filled it (Uncle Al's life is based largely on believing things like that; please don't tell him otherwise), and knowing that he could never produce a one-piece wooden wedge as thick as a door and that slanted just the right amount, on trip No. 2 he bought a bunch of shims that were about the right width, along with some glue, nails and wood filler.

(To those who would decry this wood-and-glue-and-filler method as amateurish, and to those who would say it was more work than just cutting one piece of wood to fit, Uncle Al would say "Epoxy on both your houses.")

Anyway, he glued together a wedge-shaped thing (herein-after, the "thing") and nailed it to the underside of the top of the door frame. He decided that it didn't look bad sticking down from the door frame unless you looked at it. (Yes; again, please don't tell him.)

He had positioned it carefully so it lined up along the top of the door frame, so it would be directly above the door when it was closed.

He was pleased that although he had neglected to consider whether the house was out of plumb (and, for that matter, whether he was out of chocolate—in the short run a bigger problem), he had recovered fairly easily. So he proceeded to drill the latch hole into the door frame at the right height and centered in the frame.

In hindsight, he could have marked the position of that hole when he was positioning the "thing," or (very improbably) he could have thought, "Since there were no right angles in the doorway opening as seen head-on, what makes me think that, viewed from the top, the top of the door frame is parallel with the bottom of the door frame?"

Of course, he did neither, and of course, it wasn't: When the door was centered in the frame at the door handle, the wedgy "thing" that was parallel to the top of the frame slanted out over the top of the door. The end of it stuck out about an inch.

Over the next several days, by repeated redrilling, rehanging, and repositioning of the strike plate opening, the hinges, and the "thing," Uncle Al was able to achieve a compromise in which no part of the door fit right, but none was much worse than any of the others.

Then he began to install the molding that the closed door rests against (and that he forgot to buy on either of his first two trips).

Uncle Al shouldn't need to say that despite having painfully recognized that the door frame was out of whack in two different ways, he nonetheless assumed it was *in* whack in yet another way, so he installed the first strip of molding parallel to the edge of the door frame instead of fitting it against the door.

Of course when he angrily pried it off after he realized his error, it split, necessitating trip No. 4.

Uncle Al maintains that the separate trip to the store for paint (and the one after that, because he was wrong in believing he had a brush—or, more accurately, in believing that he could find the brush he had) really shouldn't count against the door project.

A final note, for the record: In the two days that Uncle Al had the door off later, to paint it, Fuzzy had pity on him and stole only one doughnut.

Your Pre-Op Checklist

I just heard about a fellow who was going to have a coronary artery bypass and was instructed to shave his chest at home before the surgery.

Between having patients prep themselves for surgery and having them give themselves IVs at home after they get kicked out of the hospital, there is an uncomfortable "where will it stop?" feeling.

Presenting the Pre-Op Checklist, from just a few years in the future:

Thank you for choosing OptiSick MedCaring Corp.

We want the experience of having someone fishing around in your abdominal cavity to be a pleasant one. If you have suggestions as to how we might make your visit more enjoyable, please make a note on the back of this sheet and leave it on the emergency-room door.

The night before your surgery:

- Eat no food after 8 p.m.; drink nothing after midnight. Every hour on the hour, from 10 p.m. until you can't believe it anymore, administer one of the attached five king-size doses of Gut-Be-Kleen. You may experience fatigue after the final (2 a.m.) dose.
- There is nobody on duty after 8 p.m. If you have

questions about the procedure that will be performed, consult a medical reference book.

- Between doses of Gut-Be-Kleen, remove all body
hair (except on scalp and face) with a razor, and
wipe down with the attached depilatory cream.
How old are you? Well, that's how long it'll take you
to grow all that again! (That's a joke that the folks
who used to shave you in the hospital used to make.
We thought you were entitled to hear it even if those
folks have been laid off.)

- For appendectomy patients: Locate McBurney's
Point (two-thirds of the way between the umbili-
cus—that's the belly button to you, sport—and the
right hip), and gently mark it on your belly with
the attached indelible pen. Yes, it hurts. That's why
we said gently.

- For gallbladder patients: Punch yourself here and
there with a pointed finger. Indicate where it hurts
with the attached indelible pen. (Appendectomy
patients, do not try this, or at least nail mattress to
ceiling first.)

- For hernia patients: Use the attached indelible pen
to mark with a single large X the side on which your
hernia is located. Do not attempt to play Tic-Tac-
Toe, as this tends to confuse the surgeons.

All surgery patients:

- Produce a urine specimen in the attached cup,
then test (see attached sheet) for protein, glucose,

pregnancy, heroin addiction and poppyseed-muffin consumption.

- Stick yourself in the arm with the attached needle (keep trying; you'll find a vein eventually). NOTE: DO NOT CONFUSE NEEDLE WITH THE AT-TACHED INDELIBLE PEN. SURGICAL REMOVAL OF INDELIBLE PEN FROM YOUR ARM WILL RESULT IN EXTRA CHARGES ON YOUR BILL.

- Draw approximately 10 cubic centimeters of blood and run the tests specified on the attached sheet, following instructions on that sheet. Be sure to return lab instruments to the hospital when you report for surgery. FAILURE TO RETURN CENTRIFUGE, AUTOCLAVE AND SPECTROMETER WILL RE-SULT IN EXTRA CHARGES ON YOUR BILL.

- Following directions on the attached sheet for your particular kind of surgery, use the attached scalpel to perform the initial incision, then immediately close with attached Ticky-Tacky Tape. This will give us a head start on your surgery, and the sooner we're done, the sooner we can all go home. (Do not be concerned about bleeding; we've seen lots of messy work.)

- Report to Admitting at 5:30 a.m. There will be no-body there yet, and no surgery is performed before, oh, say, 9:30, but the earlier you drag yourself in, the more exhausted you'll be, and the easier it will be for us to knock you out. FAILURE TO BEAT US TO THE DOOR WILL BE NOTED, AND EXCESS ANESTHESIA REQUIRED BECAUSE YOU SLEPT LATE WILL RESULT IN EXTRA CHARGES ON YOUR BILL.

Your medical team is composed of professionals. Do not pester them with questions if your surgery does not begin at the time indicated. Medical emergencies and interesting guests on *Donahue* sometimes cause delays. Doctors have patients; we ask that you have patience, too. (Hippocrates told that one to his nurse; isn't it cute?)

Please don't ask nurses or doctors for food or drink immediately after your surgery; there are snack and pop machines in the alcove of each room. Bring coins when you come to the hospital; nurses do not carry change.

Checkout typically is less than two hours after surgery is completed; that way we don't have to listen to you moan when the anesthetic wears off.

OptiSick MedCaring Corp. is a division of Impervia Cost Management Group, a member of the Health Plan Alliance, part of and indistinguishable from the Professional Clinic System Partners Association. Try and guess who to call.

Fuzzy's Daytime Cereal Episode

≺≺≺

Last fall Uncle Al introduced two major changes into his life: He adopted Fuzzy, a long but short dog; and he started piano lessons. Because two big changes in one season are approximately 100 times his preferred pace, it makes sense at this point to report on the progress Uncle Al is making on mastering the piano and the progress Fuzzy is making on mastering Uncle Al.

The first report can be brief, and it offers an immediate transition to the second:

Uncle Al isn't doing too badly on the piano (considering that he dropped his first attempt to beat the instrument into submission after two or three months when he was in second grade, more than 50 years ago). But Fuzzy hates Uncle Al's practicing.

"So what?" some readers might ask. "Why would you care whether your dog enjoys your piano playing?" That will be addressed shortly.

But there are readers who would go beyond that, asking, "Why would anyone care at all about any of this?" To those of that number for whom this is a first exposure to the Uncle Al column, Uncle Al offers his gratitude for their curiosity—and their courage in reading this far—but he believes that this question reveals a fundamental misunderstanding of the nature of the Uncle Al enterprise. He suggests that in their search for sensible amusement they should turn to the comics, the editorial page or the obituaries.

As for returning readers who nonetheless ask why anyone would care about any of this, Uncle Al can only observe that these folks need to stop hoping that this column will someday get better—or to stop beating themselves for reading it anyway; he suggests a course of Flagyl or some other antiflagellant.

At long last, let's begin: Uncle Al is happy to report that his new pal isn't as demanding of constant affection as he was at first. (Uncle Al must acknowledge that he also is a little sad to report that his new pal isn't as demanding of constant affection as he was at first.) Fuzzy still whimpers when Uncle Al stops petting him—and baps at the nonpetting hand with a paw or his head, whichever is closer—but he does spend a fair amount of time in what might be called independent activity (if it weren't that the "activity" involved is sleeping).

He is still pretty jealous of Uncle Al's time, though. On returning from the walk he and Uncle Al take as soon as Uncle Al gets home every evening, Fuzzy's first move is not to run to the kitchen to be fed but to run upstairs and lie down on Uncle Al's bed, where he waits briefly (apparently hoping Uncle Al will join him) before he comes back downstairs for his dinner.

It is a very nice gesture, but lest you say "Awww" too fervidly, Uncle Al notes that Fuzzy's dinner is a bowl of dog food, just like his breakfast; it's not as if he were forgoing a banquet. And if Uncle Al took him up on the offer and went to bed at 6 p.m., it's entirely possible that Fuzzy would go downstairs at 6:05 and eat his bowl of dog food.

Fuzzy's only bad habit—his preference for turning bags of doughnuts and the like, left where he can reach them, into bags of no doughnuts and the like, on the floor—has been far less evident since Uncle Al installed the kitchen door. Uncle Al closes the door when he isn't home, leaving Fuzzy in the part of the house notable for its lack of doughnuts and the like.

That this bad habit hasn't disappeared altogether is Uncle Al's fault—occasionally he forgets to close the door, and sometimes he carelessly leaves a grocery item outside the kitchen.

Recently, for example, he brought home three bags of groceries. Two included perishables, and he rushed them to the kitchen and put everything away. He somehow forgot about the third bag, which he left on a living room chair and didn't notice the next morning when he left for work. It contained a box of cereal, some glass cleaner, a box of plastic garbage bags and paper towels.

When he came home that evening, Uncle Al found the bag tipped over, the other items untouched, but the cereal box and its inner plastic bag chewed through, some cereal strewn around, more of it clearly missing, and a very nervous-looking Fuzzy.

(Uncle Al prefers to believe that Fuzzy can sniff cereal through a sealed plastic bag inside a closed cardboard box, not that Fuzzy was able to conclude from a glance at the nutrition label that he might enjoy the cereal more than the garbage bags.)

OK, that's how Fuzzy is in general: slightly challenging but pretty darn swell.

On the matter of the piano, though, Fuzzy is beginning to be a bit of a pain.

He used to ignore Uncle Al's nightly practice, but for the past few months, whenever Uncle Al sits down to play, Fuzzy comes over and begins to whimper. Sometimes he gives up fairly soon and lies down, defeated.

But on other occasions (Uncle Al doesn't know what the

additional impetus might be—dislike of a particular chord? a particular tune? a particular composer?), Fuzzy raises the stakes by bonking Uncle Al's arm with his head, and he has actually jumped up onto the piano bench several times and tried to stand across Uncle Al's lap, effectively concluding the concert.

Uncle Al is pretty sure that this is not Fuzzy just wanting to sit in Uncle Al's lap and be petted. No, there is a clear connection to the music, because nothing happens until Uncle Al starts to play.

And, now that he thinks about it, Uncle Al is pretty sure it didn't happen at all until he installed the kitchen door. What could that mean? Hmmm . . .

Yike!!

It's unlikely, but it would make sense: By whining and bonking Uncle Al's arm when he practices, Fuzzy could well be trying to say, "If I have to listen to this, couldn't I at least have a doughnut?"

Mustn't Knock Tomato Opportunity

ᴖᴖᴖ

In the past, Uncle Al has groused about junk mail, junk e-mail, and even about misdirected instant messages in Spanish from somebody who thought Uncle Al was Alberto Simons and lived in Peru.

Now, Uncle Al is happy to report, a delightful variation just showed up in the Taste section's e-mail box. (Uncle Al combs that occasionally, looking for any actual correspondence that might be hidden among the offers of instant wealth, instant refinancing, instant sex and instant coffee.)

It was business-to-business e-mail from one Ken Feng, probably sent to lots of firms. Uncle Al assumes the Taste section was included because Feng has some software that decided that "Taste" might be a grocery manufacturer.

This is the entire peculiar message, except for contact information, which a kindly Uncle Al has excluded, to keep Upper Midwest pranksters from phoning Feng in the middle of the night:

"Dear sir, We have about 500MT tomato paste 36/38% cold break Crop 2003 for sales. If you are interested, pls contact us immediately. B.Rgds, Ken Feng/Sales Manager Guangzhou Youbao Industry Co., Ltd."

Uncle Al guessed, correctly (that's why he gets the medium bucks), that MT is metric tons. From the Internet he learned that "36/38% cold break" refers to the amount of tomato in the paste and how it was heat-treated. Guangzhou is the place in China we used to call Canton (although how anybody got Canton out of Guangzhou is a good question—unless Guangzhou is pronounced "Canton").

And what can Uncle Al say about the e-mail? An offer of 500 metric tons of tomato paste doesn't come every day—although the way e-mail is going it might not be too long before offers like that come several times a minute.

It certainly was intriguing, but Uncle Al had a few questions. For one, he didn't quite recall the density of tomato paste. (Just how much room does 500 metric tons of it take up?)

And if it isn't all in 6-ounce cans, which he doubted it was, what is it in? A barge? A giant plastic bag? That would be a real mess to keep around.

And then there's the perennial tomato paste problem: No recipe ever calls for the whole container. If you start with 500 metric tons, when you're done there's always 150 or 200 metric tons in the bottom of the barge and you're stuck trying to find ways to use it up.

On the other hand, Uncle Al has been known to pass up just this kind of chance and then to regret it endlessly. This could easily become "the time he didn't buy the tomato paste." So he decided to explore the matter just a bit.

A metric ton is about 2,200 pounds, so 500 metric tons is about 1.1 million pounds. By looking at other Web sites where tomato paste is for sale in metric-ton quantities (ain't technology grand?) (and ain't commerce strange?), Uncle Al determined that the common containers seem to be 300-gallon bins and 55-gallon drums. In each case the container is lined with (Uncle Al guessed it!) . . . a giant plastic bag.

A 300-gallon bin weighs about 2,900 pounds when full of tomato paste, so (ignoring the weight of the bin itself), 500 metric tons of tomato paste would be about 380 bins. Since a 300-gallon bin of tomato paste is 52.9 cubic feet, including the bin (a handy fact to file away), the whole pile would take up 20,100 cubic feet.

Uncle Al determined that that would be a cube of tomato paste 27.2 feet on a side, but he couldn't really picture that. So he tried another approach. He calculated that in a pile 8 feet high, 20,100 cubic feet of bins of tomato paste would take up about 2,510 square feet—a square 50.1 feet on a side. Still not quite graspable.

Then he got it: 500 metric tons of tomato paste will fill a 2,500-square-foot house, floor to 8-foot ceiling, and leave 80 cubic feet of tomato paste—a few hundred gallons—for kids to play with in the yard.

To ensure that 2,500 square feet was a reasonable size house to visualize, he turned again to that paragon of information and distraction, the Internet. He learned that 2,500 square feet is just a bit bigger than the average new house—and that he could rent one room in a 2,500-square-foot house with a pool and a putting green "close to shopping, restaurants and route 51" for $395 a month ("Call Crystal"). It turned out to be in Phoenix.

Back to tomato paste: Other than being "36/38% cold break," Feng's tomato paste seemed to be generic—no herbs or seasonings to make it notable or attractive. (Oh, OK; Uncle Al will say it: So much tomato paste, so little thyme.) So the potential opportunity was strictly about price—and Feng hadn't said what he was asking.

Uncle Al was only looking, so he didn't want to ask Feng, as any contact might lead to lots more e-mail offers. So he poked around at a few giant international commodities sites on the

Internet and found several tomato paste offers in the range of $600 to $700 per metric ton, depending on packaging, from such places as China, Ghana and Iran. That's around 30 cents a pound, plus freight.

A 6-ounce can goes for at least 49 cents in supermarkets (that's $1.31 a pound). Feng sounded desperate; if he would take $500 a metric ton (about 23 cents a pound), this could be a really good deal.

All Uncle Al would have to do is raise $250,000 (plus freight), remove all the furniture and belongings from his house (and garage; his house is less than 2,500 square feet), make all the doors and windows tomato-paste-tight, and sit back and wait for the profits to roll in.

But where would he live? He might well call Crystal.

Stress Test Stresses Testing

ʻʻʻ

Now it can be told: Uncle Al recently cheated death twice.

A couple of weeks ago, he found himself trotted off to the hospital because he was exhibiting almost every indication of a heart attack except screaming, "I'm having a heart attack!" It turned out, apparently, to be merely some kind of digestive upset.

As Charles Dickens would have put it, were he recasting *A Christmas Carol* and substituting Uncle Al for Marley's ghost, "There was more of heartburn than of heart about it."

Or maybe "more of Fudgsicle than of ventricle." Or "more of torta than of aorta." Or "more of celeriac than of cardiac." Or "more of huckleberry than of coronary." Or "more of confection than of infarction." Or "more of [Slap!!]"

Thank you. Uncle Al needed that.

All of that notwithstanding (and not with sitting, either— Uncle Al departed the newsroom horizontally on a cart), whatever it was that happened to Uncle Al provided a few minutes' welcome entertainment for his colleagues, and it got him out of what had promised to be a particularly unenjoyable meeting later that day.

In any case, Uncle Al is as fit as whatever kind of fiddle is somewhat overweight, doesn't exercise much and is inordinately fond of snack foods, butter, cream, eggs and chocolate.

This was confirmed not only by the absence in his blood of any indication of a recent heart attack (at least, any indication that wasn't obscured by large amounts of creme filling), but also by his having passed what is euphemistically called a "stress test," which was administered the next morning.

(Uncle Al got to stay in the hospital overnight, which actually would have been rather pleasant, as he was given excellent and attentive care throughout his visit, but he missed several of his favorite cheesy reruns on TV because the set in his room didn't get Fox.

(And he had to call and ask a friend to go to his house to walk Fuzzy, who seemed to be rather put out by this development—so much, in fact, that he left his dinner in his dish until Uncle Al returned the next day. Uncle Al likes to think of this as a demonstration of Fuzzy's loyalty, as opposed to evidence of how little it takes to upset him.)

Uncle Al noted to the medical folks that he didn't need to take a stress test because he has one every day at work, but this was said to be a different kind, and there was no getting out of it.

It consists of running uphill on an increasingly fast-moving treadmill (which Uncle Al would insist really is pretty much like every day at work), while hooked up to a cardiac monitor. Apparently the idea is that if you haven't already had a heart attack, they might as well see what it takes to give you one.

No, no: They don't really try to make you have a heart attack. Uncle Al is merely using the humor mechanism known as exaggeration or sarcasm or something. They just try to see if the combined stress of a 6 a.m. wake-up (to be weighed), breakfast on the low-salt version of hospital food, running uphill on an increasingly fast treadmill and being pretty sure your gown is coming open in back is enough to make you start having chest pains.

Uncle Al must point out, both in fairness and because it's hilarious, that although he was made to pant uphill for several minutes on an increasingly fast treadmill while pretty sure that his gown was coming open in back, he was transported to and from the test in a wheelchair.

Well, he passed the test and, as he started to say earlier, all of that now is safely behind him.

He wanted to wait at least a week to mention it, to get past the second potentially fatal danger—what he has been thinking of as "the irony phase."

That's the period of a week or so after his release from the hospital, during which, if he keeled over in the parking lot, without doubt someone in the crowd gathering around as he turned blue would say, "Boy, is this ironic: He just had a stress test at the hospital last week!"

"Actually," Uncle Al would certainly attempt to point out from the pavement, "this is merely a case of strikingly unfortunate coincidence. It isn't irony unless something that the hospital did in treating me for a possible heart attack *caused* me to drop dead of a heart attack. As it is, it . . ."

And that, he has feared, is when he would be fatally set upon with stones.

Look! Everywhere! It's Ted!

ͯͯͯ

Uncle Al recently brought folks up to date on his fine new dog, Fuzzy, who has shared Uncle Al's doughnuts for more than a year now, so maybe it's time to stop calling him new.

Readers who take careful notes on these things, perhaps fearing that there could one day be a quiz, might recall that Fuzzy appeared in Uncle Al's life to fill part of the void left by the departure of the swell dog Lucky, who roomed with Uncle Al on and off for more than fifteen years. Fifteen years is longer than both of Uncle Al's marriages put together: If Lucky had had opposable thumbs instead of dewclaws, Uncle Al would have given him a set of house keys.

Another part of that Luckyless void was filled when Lucky's owner adopted an enthusiastic little dog named Teddy, who looks, at least from the top, pretty much like a mop from which someone has removed the handle. And now whenever Teddy's owner is out of town, Teddy bunks with Uncle Al and Fuzzy.

Uncle Al notes that Teddy's visits are very different from Lucky's.

For one thing, Lucky was fairly relaxed. (He made exceptions from this policy in order to make a great deal of noise during visits from mail carriers, UPS guys and pizza deliverers, but Uncle Al doesn't think his heart was really in it.) Fuzzy, too, except for demanding his share of doughnuts (and his preference for constant petting and no piano playing) exhibits a low-key—one might say companionable—demeanor.

Teddy seems to have attended the other school. When Uncle Al chose, just now, to describe him as "enthusiastic," he had many other options, all equally valid. Among them are "earnest," "joyous," "manic" and "cranked."

When Uncle Al gets home from work, Fuzzy wags and whimpers and begs to be petted.

Teddy leaps straight up in the air.

About three feet.

Repeatedly.

He's not very big; if he were Fuzzy's size, they would be six- or seven-foot leaps. It's a performance that is at once impressive, gratifying and a little scary.

When he's out for a walk, Teddy investigates not only every tree that Fuzzy investigates but many trees that Fuzzy doesn't. All those extra tree stops make Teddy fall behind Fuzzy and Uncle Al (Uncle Al generally does not stop to sniff any trees), but Teddy catches up after each tree by hurling himself at the next one. During this speeding-bullet imitation, his long hair streams out behind him, reminding Uncle Al of the blowing-necktie ads for Maxell audiotape.

This is Teddy's typical mode of self-propulsion at home, too. So if, for example, Uncle Al is reading the newspaper and Teddy is on the other side of the room, Teddy can fling himself into Uncle Al's lap in what seems to be a single bound—under, around or straight through the newspaper.

(Again, it's a good thing Teddy is small—he weighs about 10 pounds. If he were Fuzzy's size, Uncle Al would be writing this from the hospital.)

To tell the truth, all of this (although it might not sound like it) is really quite adorable, at least in limited doses. To his credit, Ted isn't at all yappy. And much of his enthusiasm on these sleepovers is directed into trying to be as close to Uncle Al as possible. When he finally winds down, he can be as cuddly as Fuzzy.

On those occasions Uncle Al is able to make himself a dog-bread sandwich, with one arm on each of them, petting. He can't so much as read a book, though, because holding it would mean that one or both dogs would be getting only a draped-over elbow instead of a full forearm commitment, with constant head stroking. Both dogs regard the elbow deal as unacceptable.

But such relaxed moments are in the minority, and the rest of the Teddy Show—All Ted, All the Time—can be a little weary-ing. Uncle Al sometimes describes him as an adorable dog who could benefit from a central-nervous-system depressant.

Ted's presence is a little hard on Fuzzy, too, as keeping Ted from his almost continuous attempts to climb Uncle Al requires Uncle Al to divide the attention that Fuzzy strongly prefers to be undivided.

Other than that, the boys seem to get along pretty well. Fuzzy occasionally struts around with one of Teddy's toys, clearly trying to get a rise out of him. And Teddy occasion-ally picks a fight with Fuzzy on similar principles. But they act more or less in concert when they're out for a walk together.

Which raises directly another significant difference be-tween Lucky's vacations with Uncle Al and Teddy's: When Teddy visits Uncle Al, Uncle Al has two dogs.

Walking two dogs is not twice as difficult as walking one. But neither is it, as one acquaintance suggested it might be, twice the chick magnet. From one point of view it is about half the chick magnet, as at any moment there is twice the chance that one of the dogs will be tending to the very business for which they are being walked in the first place. Although most people understand this, it does detract from the moment's potential chick-magnetude.

And although Uncle Al isn't exactly in the chick-magnet business, other guys might be, so for their benefit he feels he must compare the chick-magnet potential of two dogs with the only other thing in his life alleged to have that property: the purple pinstriped swoosh on the door that replaced the door he wrecked when he let his truck roll out of the garage with that door open.

(Uncle Al knows that was supposed to be a chick magnet because, in answer to Uncle Al's dismayed cry of "Purple!" that's what the auto salvage guy said, the two words separately, each with a knowing nod of his head.)

The swoosh attracted no chicks before Uncle Al removed it, so he cannot be sure, but he judges that it was a worse chick magnet than the two dogs at their most delightful—Fuzzy being adoring and Teddy leaping three feet in the air—and a better one than the two dogs at their least delightful—competing to see which one can go the most nuts because a block away one of them has spotted—good heavens—another dog!

There is one more significant difference between Ted's visits and Lucky's—and you can trust Uncle Al that it is the most welcome of the three:

When Uncle Al goes to Ted's house to pick him up, his colleagues don't make jokes about Uncle Al "getting Teddy tonight."

Dealing with a Bad Hobbit

 ·᠆ᠸᠸ᠆·

With the Academy Awards almost upon us, Uncle Al is so racked by indecision that he can hardly contain himself—although loosening his belt seems to help.

Here's what he has been agonizing about: Although it would seem that everyone in the solar system is absolutely enchanted by *Lord of the Rings*—it got a near-record 13 Oscar nominations—Uncle Al thought it was the most endlessly boring movie he'd ever seen.

He's pretty sure that this view places him in a tiny minority—*Lord of the Rings* has already earned more than a quarter of a billion dollars. But he's used to having unpopular opinions (he likes onion-and-garlic ice cream), so that's not what troubles him.

He's sure that jumping onto the Middle Earth bandwagon by making a similar movie is (finally) his sure ticket to a nice personal fortune. But to assure that he's really on the bandwagon, he believes, his movie must stick to the *Lord of the Rings* formula—in other words, it, too, must be stupendously boring.

So there it is: Wealth or artistic integrity? Wealth or artistic integrity?

Hmmm . . .

Uncle Al hopes he's made his screenplay boring enough to earn him a million dollars; it certainly doesn't have any integrity:

Lard of the Wings

(Fade in: Idyllic scene in the Wabbit village of West Bleemington. A block party is in progress, and all the Wabbits are frolicking. One charming older inhabitant calls aside his equally charming nephew.)

BOZO BAGGIES: Here, young Bongo, is a magical bottomless chicken wing. Regard it well, for it's really tasty. It has been in a drawer for half a century, behind my socks, where none would care to look.

Through the long years that it lay hidden there in safety it bothered no one, but lately I fear that others—unspeakably evil others—have begun to smell it, and they hope to capture it.

Now therefore it is for you to keep it from evil by returning it to the boiling animal fat in the magic deep fryer from which it came, way the heck north across the land, near the Range of Iron, in the village of Dool-Ooth.

BONGO BAGGIES: I'd rather not.

BOZO BAGGIES: It grieves me to place this burden upon you, young Bongo, but I am feeble with age and elderliness, and I'm not all that bright, so Jeen-O, the ancient wizard of Dool-Ooth, could easily defeat me. And this task is horrendously important: Should you fail, and allow Jeen-O to recapture the magical chicken wing . . . [He shudders.] If you fail, young Bongo, Jeen-O will cover the earth with canned chow mein for a thousand years.

BONGO BAGGIES: Yike!

BOZO BAGGIES: And I must warn you: Throughout your entire journey you will be set upon by hordes of ferocious and altogether hideous monsters, each more terrifying than the last—and each featuring even-more-disgusting special effects, too. They will stop at nothing to wrest the wing and its magic from you, and they are already magical as heck.

Beware of Jeen-O and his slavering creations, young Bongo: They bad!

BONGO BAGGIES: OK.

BOZO BAGGIES: Did I mention that the monsters will be attacking by the thousands? You had best take along five or six friends.

BONGO BAGGIES: OK.

BOZO BAGGIES [calling out to the departing Bongo]: Remember: The chow mein would be mostly celery!

BONGO BAGGIES [fading, behind ominous music]: OK.

(Fade in; Bongo Baggies and his assorted friends—Gilligan, The Professor, Bugs [another Wabbit], Uncle Fester and Thing—are hiking north across Frid-Lee. It's pretty scary. Suddenly, thousands of slavering, icky, hideous creatures come at them from every side. A titanic battle rages.)

BONGO BAGGIES: Oof!

THE PROFESSOR: Aargh!

GILLIGAN: Yipe!

(Then, as suddenly as it began, the battle is over—and Bongo and his friends are inexplicably victorious. Fade [ominous music] to the River of Elk, where Bongo and his friends are hiking north. It's pretty scary. Suddenly, thousands of slavering, icky, hideous creatures even worse than the previous ones—these are Day-Glo green and have runny noses—come at them from every side. A titanic battle rages.)

BONGO BAGGIES: Yipe!

THE PROFESSOR: Oof!

GILLIGAN: Aargh!

(Then, as suddenly as it began, the battle is over—and

Bongo and his friends are inexplicably victorious. Fade [ominous music] to Cam Bridge, where Bongo and his friends are arguing. It's pretty scary.)

BONGO BAGGIES: We are lost! We should have followed the sign of the thirty and five!

THE PROFESSOR: The sixty and five!

GILLIGAN: The ninety and four!

(Suddenly, thousands of slavering, icky, hideous creatures even worse than the previous ones—these have garlic breath from their dinner salads—come at them from every side. A titanic battle rages.)

BONGO BAGGIES: Aargh!

THE PROFESSOR: Yipe!

GILLIGAN: Oof!

(Then, as suddenly as it began, the battle is over—and Bongo and his friends are inexplicably victorious. Fade [ominous music] to Hink-Lee, where Bongo and his friends are hiking north. It's pretty scary. Bongo stops.)

BONGO BAGGIES: Something—I don't know what—tells me we're in for some trouble.

(Suddenly, thousands of slavering, icky, hideous creatures even worse than the previous ones—these are singing "Stardust"—come at them from every side. A titanic battle rages.)

BONGO BAGGIES: Oy!

THE PROFESSOR: Feh!

GILLIGAN: Ick!

(Then, as suddenly as it began, the battle is over—and Bongo and his friends are inexplicably victorious.)

THE PROFESSOR: Bongo Baggies, this is beginning to be tiresome, not to mention repetitive, dreary, unimaginative and boring. Even to me, and I'm a real stick!

Every time we win a battle I assume we're done. But then there's . . . another battle. How many more nearly identical battles do we face before we get to Dool-Ooth? Can't we manage to involve some other plot device than a battle with monsters? I distinctly heard snoring in the audience! How about I eat the $%@# chicken wing?

BONGO BAGGIES [sotto voce]: Shut up, Professor; we get a cut of the box office. [Aloud]: O, mighty Lord Jeen-O! Bring on your next horde of slavering, icky, hideous creatures even worse than the previous ones! We are not afraid! Indeed, O mighty Lord Jeen-O, do your worst: Let this horde of slavering, icky, hideous creatures be doing the macarena!

Life on the Slippery Slope

ᴖᴖᴖ

It's time once more to check on the progress of Uncle Al's continuing slide from reasonably sound thinker to dish of cottage cheese.

There are those, to be sure, who would say that the transformation is already complete, and others who would argue that he was never a reasonably sound thinker in the first place.

Such quibbling aside, the latest evidence is particularly irritating to Uncle Al, possibly because it comes at a time when his dog, Fuzzy, is displaying increasingly sensitive interpretational skills.

For probably 20 years Uncle Al has had a pronounced inability to remember names. Names of anything: actors, coworkers, TV shows, relatives . . . you name it; he can't.

To be precise, Uncle Al doesn't actually forget names, he simply can't come up with them on the spot. He absolutely knows, for example, the name of the person who has had the desk next to him for something like four years. He just can't name him right now.

This has come to be less annoying for Uncle Al than it used to be. For maybe 10 of the past 20 years, instead of grinding away at recalling the name of a movie or a colleague or whatever has gotten stuck on its way into what might have been brilliant conversation before Uncle Al stopped it cold, he attempts a description.

He has come so far in that regard recently that he no longer believes he can find one proper noun by searching for another. Even if he begins to say "That guy . . . you know, he was in . . . that movie with . . . that other guy," these days he tries to shift to another approach, at least when he is among friends—such folks as . . .

This is a perfect example! Instead of wasting five minutes trying to name two friends, he might say "The guy is a copy editor on the state team, the woman writes for the business section; they both eat lunch with me five days a week."

Just because he has developed this fairly adequate workaround doesn't mean that Uncle Al always uses it—or that it works in every case. It wouldn't be particularly helpful, for example, in introducing a visitor to his supervisor's supervisor's supervisor. "This is . . . ummm . . . a guy who's trying to sell me something, and this is . . . ummm . . . the editor . . . he has a Scandinavian first name—it's not Lars."

Anyway, although it is occasionally difficult to believe, this proper-noun thing hasn't gotten any worse over time. But Uncle Al keeps a watchful eye on the rest of his mental life, and he is dismayed to report the following development:

In a recent lunch conversation, although he came up effortlessly with the name he needed, it appears that he was unable to find the word "brother." Without pause—without even thinking that he was missing a word and needed a substitute— he sailed into a (very peculiar) alternate phrasing.

Seeing someone in the restaurant who looked rather like a mutual acquaintance, he said "If [so-and-so] had a kid who was older than him but looked like him, that'd be him over by the window."

Even though he recalled the full name of "so-and-so" without so much as a grunt, the rest of that sentence surely means things look bad for Uncle Al.

Fuzzy, meanwhile, is becoming more and more intuitive. His intuition isn't always correct, but he forms it quickly.

Two examples:

Fuzzy recently had an eye infection for which the vet prescribed a medication that had to be squeezed out of a tube directly onto the dog's eye, which Uncle Al had to hold open.

Fuzzy didn't care for this deal at all, and he thrashed around on the couch while Uncle Al tried to hold him still and hold his eye open—all with one hand—while squeezing the stuff into the eye. The whole thing was quite unpleasant for both of them.

For a whole week they went through this three times a day—right after morning and evening meals and at bedtime.

To keep the medication handy and to help him remember to administer it, Uncle Al kept it in his shirt pocket. One evening late in that week, well after dinner, Uncle Al sat down on the couch next to Fuzzy to do a crossword puzzle.

He reached into his pocket for a pen—and Fuzzy ran upstairs.

The other example of Fuzzy's thought process involves Uncle Al's fairly firm addiction to TV. When Uncle Al will be away during the evening and thus will miss one or two of his favorite shows, he sets the VCR to record them.

Usually he doesn't think of this until he's getting ready to leave, so he picks up the remote from the couch and stands there setting the VCR just before he puts on his coat and leaves. (Then he watches the tape in bed and falls asleep before anything happens.)

Fuzzy spends weekdays alone, perhaps dreaming of staging a sneak attack on the doughnut supply once Uncle Al comes home and opens the kitchen door. He's a quiet dog, and he barks only when something really upsets him.

On the several evenings a week that Uncle Al walks and feeds Fuzzy and then puts on his coat to leave again, Fuzzy sits down well away from the door and gets very quiet. He would prefer Uncle Al to stay home and pet him.

A recent development: If it's still daylight outside and Uncle Al points the remote at the VCR while he's standing up, Fuzzy apparently figures he'll be losing an even more unacceptable amount of petting, and he begins to bark.

Uncle Al is hoping to help Fuzzy improve his ability to communicate: He's pretty sure Fuzzy remembers the name of the editor.

Beyond the Pail

A few weeks ago, a colleague who was cleaning his desk tossed me a government document that had come to the newspaper, unsolicited, in the mail. The 130-page, 8⅜- by10¾-inch paperback, a publication of the U.S. International Trade Commission, bore the enchanting title *Certain Steel Pails From Mexico.* I read it avidly.

It proved to be a report on allegations that imported steel pails were being sold in the United States for less than their fair value, and that such sales were harming the American steel pail industry. Pail dumping, as it were.

You might have missed this volume, but perhaps you read the riveting *Certain Residential Door Locks and Parts Thereof from Taiwan* and the shocking *Certain Electrical Conductor Aluminum Redraw Rods from Venezuela,* both cited in *Certain Steel Pails.*

I bet you're thinking that *Certain Steel Pails* sounds boring— that there's not a single chuckle in the entire volume. You would lose that bet. In fact, it is hilarious. I'm thinking of subscribing to the series.

It begins by defining steel pails at some length (they are made of steel, they are round, etc.), and proceeds to differentiate them from plastic pails (the latter are made of plastic, are not made by welding, are less likely to dent, are used to hold different things, etc.). In short, it sounds very close to what a C-average high-school senior would do to pad out his term paper about a visit to a steel pail factory.

There follow four heavily footnoted pages defending the decision that the industry affected by the import of steel pails from Mexico is the U.S. steel pail industry, not the U.S. plastic pail industry. Yow.

The best part is the appendices, where the evidence is laid out. Just how bad, for example, was the dumping by Envases, the only Mexican pail manufacturer involved? The Department of Commerce "examined U.S. sales of Envases totaling * * * pails, with a gross value of $ * * *. Of these, * * * percent, by volume, and * * * percent, by value, were found to be sold at LTFV [less than fair value]."

That's right, the numbers are censored from the report. And it goes on like that, with asterisks flying, for more than 50 pages.

"What the hey?" you are probably asking yourself.

Good question.

We could save countless tax dollars if the commission didn't bother printing thousands of copies of this treatise and just faxed a note saying "You won" or "You lost" to the four or five people who cared.

But all the deletions aroused my curiosity. I decided to check into the matter of certain steel pails from Mexico for myself, using the method pioneered by Dr. Dale Helman, Monterey, California.

Helman is the 32-year-old neurologist who attended the Super Bowl in Minneapolis to get a $10,000 tax write-off. He paid $1,550 apiece for four tickets on the 50-yard line, rented a Rolls for $2,000 a day and said he'll write the trip off because he took three pals to the game and planned to discuss neurology with them at halftime.

I could use a tax write-off, too, I thought, so I rounded up a bunch of friends and took off for Acapulco. Oh, all right, we were going on vacation anyway, but now I had a reason to go—and to take my friends.

One day we went to the central market, where I purchased a certain steel pail. It was made in Mexico City. It cost me 10,000 pesos (about $3.32). I did not haggle with the seller since I wanted a big tax write-off, so that price might be a little high.

Later, I discussed the price with a guide in the market—a talk that, I point out to potential auditors of my tax return, I could not have had if I had not gone to Mexico. "Ten thousand is good price," he said. "Is metal." I stopped him before he could elaborate on the differences between steel pails and plastic pails or get into certain electrical conductor aluminum redraw rods.

Instead, we went to see a seller of small jewelry, a man named Juan, from whom I purchased a certain nickel bracelet for my son Dave. (No, it was made of nickel. It cost something like $12. It differed in several important respects from certain plastic bracelets being sold elsewhere in the market.)

Later, back at our villa, my friends and I discussed the whole steel pail matter at great tax-deductible length. To further my investigation, we decided, I must travel, tax-deductible, to Mexico City, where Envases is headquartered, to price certain steel pails at their source.

Other trips will surely be needed. My investigation is just beginning; I will let you know how things proceed, but the process is really wearing me out. Already I have found myself pail and Juan.

No Man Is an Eyelet

One morning a few weeks ago as I was tying my shoes, preparatory to launching myself out the front door to see (borrowing Dorothy Parker's phrase) what fresh hell the new day would bring, one of the laces snapped.

I wasn't surprised: These are my favorite shoes; I wear them every day with almost no exception, and laces give out under those circumstances. I retied the shoe with what remained of the shoelace and made a mental note to get a new pair of laces before the one on the other shoe gave out.

In general, my mental notes aren't worth the mental paper they're printed on, and this one was no exception. A week or so later, pretty much on schedule, the other shoelace snapped. I laced that shoe with a partial lace, too, and made another mental note.

"Go to the drugstore and get shoelaces before the second wear point on either of these partial laces snaps," read that mental note. I seem to have kept the mental carbon, because I can recall making the mental note, but I must have misplaced the mental original because I never went to the drugstore and I was still using those partial shoelaces (and tying very tiny knots) when, sure enough, a week or so later what was left of the lace on one of the shoes snapped.

That propelled me to the drugstore on my way to work that very day because there was no longer enough lace to go through more than one pair of eyelets, and even then I couldn't tie a bow in the knot. The shoe was half flopping off my foot with each step, and I knew it would be only a matter of time before the other shoe was in the same condition.

I spent several minutes wandering up and down the drug-store aisles (step-schlup, step-schlup, step-schlup) past a be-wildering array of hair-care products, nail-care products and tooth-care products. If you want to worry about where our country is headed, take a look some time at how many kinds of toothbrushes we can choose among. After passing the skin-care products, nose-care products, and parts-of-us-I-can't-even-mention-care products, I arrived, finally, at the rack of shoelaces.

I noted immediately two things: There were lots more choices than I wanted to deal with—besides length and color there also were round or flat, leather or fabric and I think something else (but now I can't imagine what)—and there were almost no brown laces.

After lots of poking around behind the black laces and the white ones, I found, shoehorned in, a pair of brown, round 27-inch fabric laces. Boy, I thought; it's getting harder and harder to find the simplest stuff.

When I got to work (step-schlup, step-schlup, step-schlup), I plopped into my chair, removed the bedraggled bits of lace from both shoes and laced them up with the new ones. Ahhh. Much better.

Something was wrong about them, though.

It took me a while, but I finally figured out what:

The shoes for which I hunted and bought the brown laces, the shoes I've worn almost every day for about a year (and which are identical to the shoes I wore almost every day for a couple of years before that), the shoes I was wearing while

I was standing in the drugstore, looking high and low for the right brown laces—those shoes, dear reader, those shoes are black.

I would make a mental note to go back to the drugstore and get some black laces, and keep these brown ones as spares, but I'm a little worried about what kind of toothbrush I might wind up buying.

Fuzzy Gets Uncle Al Another Truck

Y C C

Uncle Al hasn't written about Fuzzy for a while, but not because there was nothing to tell. In fact, Uncle Al has been keeping a major problem under his hat for some time. (No, it's not his head.)

One of Fuzzy's particularly pleasant personality pluses (besides that he doesn't indulge in unnecessary alliteration) has been that he loves to ride in the truck. Uncle Al has especially enjoyed this on weekends, which are always full of errands that other folks might have handled during the week. But this isn't about Uncle Al's time-management skills.

Uncle Al found Fuzzy to be a very amicable vehicle companion. He (Fuzzy, not Uncle Al) would look out the window, nap or work on one of those rawhide or nylon bones, and Uncle Al felt comfortable going where he wanted, splitting a doughnut 90/10 with Fuzzy now and then, and stopping at home if he needed.

That had not been the pattern recently with Lucky. In his last years Lucky wasn't a great car rider. Rather than sit or lie down, he would stand on the seat, in constant peril of losing his balance, so Uncle Al tended to leave him home. This made Uncle Al feel guilty several times a day when, as he ducked in and out, Lucky would give him a baleful stare.

In self-protection (because Lucky seemed to have enough bale to fill up that stare whenever Uncle Al departed), Uncle Al took to avoiding natural stops at home (bathroom breaks and the like), lessening the stress on Lucky but increasing it on Uncle Al.

(Lucky's stress often found an outlet in which Uncle Al spontaneously spoke on his behalf, usually quite insultingly about Uncle Al. Not only did this made Uncle Al doubt his sanity, it also hurt his feelings. In their 2½ years together, by contrast, Fuzzy has not caused Uncle Al to utter a single word for him.)

Anyway, Uncle Al was really happy that Fuzzy proved to be a natural truck passenger.

And he was really upset when, some months ago, Fuzzy took a sudden severe dislike to the truck, trembling when he got in, whining if he stopped trembling, and being altogether so miserable that Uncle Al left him home whenever possible.

It was this serious: When Fuzzy had to come along, Uncle Al offered him dog treats, but for the first few minutes he wouldn't even look at them.

Uncle Al will never know what first set Fuzzy off, but the problem began well before Uncle Al's recent purchase of a new truck.

The previous truck had developed a coolant leak, and at a lunch discussion a few folks suggested that Uncle Al might want to take advantage of one of the zero-percent-interest deals to get a brand-new truck. He was incredulous.

Uncle Al never buys new vehicles. To the adage "Buying a used car is only buying someone else's problems" he has always responded: "And buying a new car is only buying your own problems—and paying extra."

On this occasion he added, "I've bought only one new car in my life, and it was nothing but problems."

"And when was that?" inquired one of his companions,

who surely knew the answer, as there are no stories Uncle Al hasn't told—often.

"1967," he replied.

New cars have improved in the intervening 35 years, someone suggested, adding, "You might actually enjoy having a vehicle that simply runs well."

Possibly with a vague hope that it might address Fuzzy's problem, Uncle Al had relented and bought an inexpensive new truck.

Which only made it worse.

Uncle Al tried lots of things: Following the advice of an animal-behavior expert to associate the new truck with pleasant things (like dinner), after their walk one evening he climbed into the truck with Fuzzy and pulled out a dish containing Fuzzy's evening meal.

After several minutes of trembling and whining, Fuzzy slowly ate it. A few minutes later, when he and Uncle Al went into the house, Fuzzy headed for the kitchen, bonked his regular dinner dish around and whimpered until Uncle Al gave in and . . . fed him again.

(Fuzzy's take seemed to be that whatever Uncle Al had been up to out there in the deathtrap, it wasn't dinner.)

The only thing that seemed to make what we call "the automotive experience" tolerable for Fuzzy was a back seat: On the few occasions when he rode in a friend's station wagon, Fuzzy instantly hopped in back, where, if not ecstatic, at least he wasn't in agony.

Later, back in Uncle Al's truck, Fuzzy would stare into the gap between the seats, possibly hoping the back of the truck's cab would recede. Then he'd begin to tremble.

Eventually it was too much for Uncle Al. As dumb as this

sounds—and he knows it sounds so dumb that he had planned never to write about it (but plans change)—he sold his new truck at a loss and got one with an "extended cab" and a little jump seat.

When the guy filling out the paperwork at the dealership asked, offhandedly, why Uncle Al was back so soon to get another truck, and Uncle Al told him, his face froze into a pleasant mask behind which, Uncle Al knew, was "Boy, you really meet 'em in this business!"

But when Fuzzy got into the new truck, he hopped in back and lay down. That was a couple of weeks ago, and Fuzzy has been more or less fine ever since, taking a surprisingly big load off Uncle Al's shoulders.

One recent evening, still full of relief that Fuzzy can return to being a more full-time weekend companion, Uncle Al reached down, scratched him behind the ears, and said, "Fuzzy, you're my best pal."

That's when Fuzzy spoke for the very first time: "That doesn't say much for your other pals, does it?"

Let's just see if Mr. Smarty-Dog gets 10 percent of Uncle Al's next doughnut!

It's the Ides of Tuesday

Uncle Al has a friend whose family used a made-up word for the practice of picking up the bit of fuzz that the vacuum cleaner was skipping over and putting it down somewhere else so the vacuum could take another crack at it.

Uncle Al thought of it that recently in a different context, a context that it will be his pleasure to set forth for you even now:

Once upon a time, long, long ago, when Uncle Al was getting very tired of working on his journalism master's thesis, he had nothing useful to do one day, so he dropped into the office of the *Minneapolis Tribune*, one of the two immediate forerunners of the very newspaper whence come these very words.

(Just thinking about it that way makes the hair stand up on the back of Uncle Al's ears.)

Anyway, the newspaper happened to have a chair that nobody was sitting in (or perhaps in which nobody was sitting, Uncle Al is no longer sure), and the rest is history.

Uncountable pencils—and more uncountable electrons—later, the management of the newspaper, having failed to get Uncle Al to go away, gave him a watch, on the face of which are the words "30 Years Service."

It's a nice watch—besides the time, it displays the date and the day of the week (in English or Spanish). Uncle Al hasn't really minded that nine of the hour marks fell off when he dropped it a few years ago. (They rolled around under the crystal until Uncle Al dumped them out when one of them got wedged under the hour hand.)

And he hasn't minded too much the watch's next stumble into decrepitude: The tiny metal crown on the end of the stem-winder disappeared, and what's left sometimes snags on Uncle Al's shirt (or possibly on his arm or on a passing waiter); when it then wiggles back and forth, it changes the date and day.

It's a bit more annoying that the date and day no longer roll over after midnight, but at around 7 a.m., while Uncle Al is pulling himself together to face a new day and he wants to know what day that will be.

And there's this extra complication: As the display of the day of the week changes, over the course of several minutes, from one day to the next, in between it displays the Spanish name of the previous day. As MON changes to TUE, for example, for a while it says LUN—short for "lunes," which is Monday in Spanish.

That's generally not a problem (and it would be even less a problem if it happened in the wee small hours), but on Wednesday mornings it can be.

Last week, for example, when the watch was working its way up to saying WED 24 after it said TUE 24 (the number changes some time before the day does), for a few minutes it said MAR 24. MAR is short for "martes," Spanish for Tuesday, but in Uncle Al's fragile morning condition it has more than once seemed possible to him that MAR 24 (or whatever) is March 24 (or whatever)—and that because he doesn't recall doing his income taxes, he'd better get busy.

It's kind of like the dream in which you have to take the final exam in a class you never attended.

And even after he realizes that it's a former Tuesday, probably not in March, he continues briefly to have a nagging feeling about his taxes.

You might wonder why Uncle Al has not had this unfortunate watch repaired. Several years ago, when it was simply running slow and a new battery didn't help, he took it to a jewelry repair place and was told that a cleaning would be $65.

"Yow!" he said, or something similar, and rather than spend $65 to clean a watch that probably wasn't worth lots more than that in the first place, he went to the paper's photography lab and gave it a shot with the compressed-air hose that the photographers use to clean their cameras. That did the job.

If the equivalent of dusting was $65 a few years ago, Uncle Al is pretty sure that actually fixing the watch would be prohibitively expensive, so he has been living with its increasingly erratic behavior.

But he might recently have come to the end of that road. Lately it has been running fine sometimes and slow sometimes, and it has even been stopping and starting. And a new battery hasn't helped. Because this behavior is utterly unpredictable, at almost no time is Uncle Al sure that his watch is anywhere near correct.

So unless he has a rough idea what time it is and needs to know only that it's at least what his watch says, if not later (like, is it time to go home yet?), whenever he looks at his watch he also pulls out the cell phone he carries only for emergencies (and that is thus always turned off, to save the battery). He turns it on, waits while it plays its little "hello" tune, sees what time it is, resets his watch if needed—to give it another chance to be correct—and turns the cell phone off again.

Even Uncle Al thinks that's pretty stupid.

If the air hose doesn't do it this time, Uncle Al might just put the %$@& watch down on the carpet and keep moving it until the vacuum cleaner eats it.

Brushing Up on the Supernatural

ᴖᴖᴖ

While looking away from his kitchen TV the other day, searching for a stray Little Debbie Nutty Bar lost in the clutter on the table, Uncle Al thought he heard a mention of "supernatural lip gloss."

Uncle Al has learned, by painful experience, that he is prone to misunderstand things he hears on TV—even when he's not prone. (See "30-second anniversary sale" and "forehead VCR," among others.)

So he was sure that "supernatural" must have been a reference to a really great natural lip gloss, one either made with natural ingredients or in a shade best described as "natural," and so terrific that it might be called a super natural lip gloss (four words, not three).

If not—if it was a lip gloss that was supposed to levitate tables or that would cause its wearer to speak in the voice of Jacob Marley ("I wear the lip gloss I forged in life!")—that would raise not only tables but also quite a few questions.

To see what was up, Uncle Al turned to his favorite source of consternation, the Internet, looking first for "super natural lip gloss," finding zip, and then trying "supernatural lip gloss" and being richly rewarded.

The many references to supernatural lip products all seemed to occur in the puzzling context of philosophical discussion. Was there really a serious exploration on the Internet of the deep meaning of occult-oriented lip gloss?

No, on both counts. Some of the supernatural cosmetics he found also came in superneutral (apparently a slightly different color family), and what was referred to each time was not a philosophical discussion but the products' brand name: philosophy (which apparently begins with a lowercase "p").

Uncle Al then made the serious error of checking out what other stuff (besides lip gloss) philosophy brings to the vanity. If you are a guy and, like Uncle Al, you have never seriously explored what might be going on in that interminable gap between "I'm almost ready" and "Let's go," you might find sobering an examination of some of the stuff philosophy sells.

Among the offerings most stupefying to Uncle Al were the brushes: blending brush, liner brush and crease brush (each $18), lip brush ($16), shadow brush ($20), blush brush ($25) and brow brush (a steal at $10). The whole set in a travel case was $120.

He was particularly taken by the idea of a crease brush, which (a brief side trip on the Web confirmed) is offered not only by philosophy but also by a bazillion other outfits. Uncle Al is, of course, familiar with creases—as well as wrinkles, crevices and crevasses—but if he had to brush something into one of his creases (or maybe it's to brush something out of one of his creases—he really has no idea what he's talking about here), he wouldn't have thought he needed a special tool for it.

Then there are endless bath and fragrance products, including three-in-one ultra-rich shampoo, conditioner and body wash in 23 desserty and alcoholic flavors.

Note: Uncle Al isn't using "23" as a mildly amusing exaggeration, like "a bazillion." There really are 23: apple cider, banana nut bread, blueberry pie, café au lait, chocolate chip cookies, chocolate ice cream, cinnamon buns, coconut cream pie, crumb berry pie, double-rich hot cocoa, key lime pie, lavender pound cake, lemon meringue pie, melon daiquiri, mimosa, orange sherbet, old-fashioned eggnog, pumpkin pie, raspberry sorbet, señorita margarita, strawberry milkshake, vanilla cupcake and white chocolate hazelnut; each costs $16.

Oddly, there's no mocha, tres leches or cappuccino crème brulée. Uncle Al sees a possible million-dollar idea in filling this ultra-rich shampoo, conditioner and body wash dessert gap—and an even bigger possibility in offering flavors from fully neglected parts of the menu: including ultra-rich shampoo, conditioner and body wash in pot roast, fried chicken, biscuits 'n' gravy and pan-seared bay scallops.

Philosophy does offer many products in nonfood flavors, including cosmetics called "falling in love," which also lack for capitalization and, Uncle Al assumes, have an indescribable scent (as no description is offered). Here are some of them:

Falling in love "elegant fragrance" compact ($35); falling in love topical pheromone "for a sense of well-being" ($60); falling in love "perfumed romantic spray fragrance" ($35); falling in love perfumed (but apparently not romantic) shampoo, bath and shower gel ($22); falling in love antioxidant-rich moisturizing body soufflé ($30) and falling in love shimmer set: shimmer fragrance and shimmer lotion ($45).

(Uncle Al can make a fair guess at what body soufflé is, but he hasn't a clue about shimmer fragrance and shimmer lotion, unless they provide the same vibrating visual excitement sometimes caused by a TV sportscaster's plaid jacket.)

On the many previous occasions on which he has come face-to-face with an appalling array of (to him) indistinguishable products, Uncle Al has shaken his figurative head and clucked his figurative tongue (at the same time—figurative

Uncle Al is multi-talented!), focusing simultaneous disdain and admiration on the manufacturers of, for example, the just-counted 39 flavors of Ragu red pasta sauce. (Is this a great country, or what?)

But reeling through the pile of philosophy supernatural cosmetics somehow made him instead sympathize with the half of the human race he isn't one of—or with however many members of that half feel obliged to negotiate this personal-care obstacle course.

How much simpler life would be for them, he thought, if they followed the appearance regimen of the many American men like him.

Plenty of guys, of course, have a strong interest in a variety of grooming products. But it must be said that many others follow what might be called a one-bottle-fits-all approach.

This involves stumbling across a soap or shampoo they don't particularly hate, and using it for the rest of their lives as cleanser, shampoo, conditioner, body wash, bubble bath, exfoliant, moisturizer, aftershave, cologne, mosquito repellent and machine-parts degreaser.

(And, maybe, if it's supernatural, as vampire blocker.)

Sharing the Stadium Burden

ᴪᴪᴪ

Note: *Uncle Al writes his Monday column early in the preceding week to give the first-rate Uncle Al Editing Team time to straighten it out. By the time this one appears events might have outpaced it, but he feels that his message is so important that it makes no difference if it's also useless.*

Much bally has been hooed lately about a deal to enable the Minnesota Twins, a baseball firm that plays its home games in an ancient (OK, 24-year-old) stadium, to have a new one. This week, anyway, the new one is supposed to cost $522 million.

Building a new stadium for the Twins is vital: Although the old one is two years younger than Macaulay Culkin, apparently it is even more terrible than the one it replaced.

Most (75 percent) of the new stadium ($392 million) would be financed by a sales tax of 0.15 percent in Hennepin County, a tax that would add three cents to every $20 purchase for up to 30 years, or until it's increased to build an even newer stadium.

That aside, how simple this is! Why mess it up with anything as legislatively mandated as a referendum on the tax?

Uncle Al knows there are naysayers who can't see the beauty in this plan's simplicity. So he has looked into what seems to be their biggest complaint—that the tax would be imposed only in Hennepin County. Plenty of people in Hennepin County don't go to Twins games, the naysayers say (when they aren't saying "nay"), and plenty of people in the rest of Minnesota do.

Uncle Al was briefly tempted to urge that the tax to fund 75 percent of the stadium be spread, at a lower rate, across all of Minnesota. But that, too, would be unfair: Plenty of people in Minnesota don't go to Twins games, and plenty of people in other states do.

So he's proposing that a sales tax to fund the $392 million portion of the stadium be spread across all 50 states.

In 2000, sales subject to sales tax in Minnesota were $53.2 billion. If Minnesota is average (not a great assumption but close enough, and you can't make an omelet without making assumptions), the amount of such taxable sales in the United States as a whole would be 50 times that, or $2.66 trillion.

Taxing sales of $2.66 trillion to raise $392 million in one year would require a tax of only 0.0147 percent (call it 0.015 percent or three cents on every $200 in purchases). Spreading it over 10 years would require only a 0.0015 percent tax—three cents per $2,000 in purchases.

What Nevadan or Alaskan would mind a tiny tax like that to build a swell stadium for the Twins? Nobody Uncle Al knows, that's for sure!

For that matter, why stop at the U.S. border? Baseball is a worldwide sport; let's have the whole planet pitch in!

Uncle Al assumes that taxable sales in each country would be proportional to the country's gross domestic product. (See previous assumption about assumptions.) (Hey; it's a living.)

U.S. GDP was $10.4 trillion in 2003, and worldwide GDP was $49 trillion, about 4.7 times that. So imposing the tax across the globe might bring in around 4.7 times as much revenue as taxing only Americans. That is, if everyone in the world paid, we could get a new Twins stadium with a tax of three cents on every $2,000 in purchases, not in 10 years, but in just over two years!

True, Burmese and Kenyan peasants tend not to take in many Twins games. So what? That's also true of lots of people in Hennepin County; see above.

Critics will whine that many of the world's poor are very poor and shouldn't be taxed to build a stadium. But they spend very little, so they'd pay very little sales tax: If a poor Afghani spends only $400 a year, his fair share of the Twins stadium sales tax is just three-fifths of a penny a year, for a little more than two years. That's a great deal!

Or take Bangladesh: With 0.49 percent of world GDP, its 0.49 percent stadium share is $1.9 million. The 146 million folks pay just 1.3 cents each (or, spread over 10 years, about one-eighth of a cent a year). Another terrific bargain!

And, as no Bangladeshi or Afghani has called Uncle Al to object, obviously there's no need for a referendum.

A Yard Sale That's All Wet

ϓϹϹϹ

Uncle Al has spent lots of his spare time in his basement recently, sorting through box after box that had been piled all over the floor, then emptying chaotic shelf after shelf into box after box and lugging them to where he'd sorted the other box after box(es?).

This was a task Uncle Al had planned since his son Dave's last visit, when Uncle Al had to move boxes to clear a path across the basement so Dave could get to his bedroom.

Uncle Al's dream was twofold: to elevate the level of the basement, so to speak, by removing lots of useless clutter, and to make a little cash selling useless clutter to discriminating citizens in a yard sale.

He had to stop partway through sorting box after box, because he was running out of time before the Theater of Seasons rang down its icy curtain on such outdoor frivolities as yard sales.

Uncle Al planned a Friday-Saturday sale, and all that week he spent evenings pricing stuff and hauling bags of it out to the garage. And while he was out there he also sorted the pile of stuff that had taken over the garage workbench, producing several extra bags for the sale.

(The sale was to be on Uncle Al's front lawn instead of in the garage because the garage is full of stuff he doesn't want to sell, and the leftover space isn't big enough to display the stuff he does.) (Want to.) (Sell.)

Thursday night he garaged the truck (packed full of bags to drive around to the front yard Friday morning). He felt good: He had emptied almost half the open basement area—clear back to the door to Dave's room.

Friday went very nicely. It was a beautiful day, friends from work dropped by on their lunch hour, another came by to provide food and permit him a bathroom break, and Fuzzy kept him dogged company some of the time. But Fuzzy barked at folks who struck him as particularly menacing, so sometimes he was forced to watch through the front window. (Uncle Al figured browsers didn't want Bowsers pulling at trousers.)

Uncle Al sold some stuff. But most visitors seemed to be retired folks, and he anticipated that he'd do better Saturday, when people with jobs and a taste for partial socket-wrench sets would be on the loose.

He did have to put most of the stuff back in the garage overnight, but that was easy: He put it all back into bags, loaded them into the truck and drove it around and into the garage.

When he came back into the house, he noticed that the last time he'd put Fuzzy inside he had unaccountably failed to close the kitchen door, and Fuzzy had taken advantage of this rare opportunity and had eaten an entire small bag of dog treats and half a box of Little Debbie Swiss Cake Rolls off the kitchen table (and was now hiding upstairs).

Some rain was predicted for Saturday, but Uncle Al had planned for it: After he drove everything back out to the front yard Saturday morning, he arranged a long sheet of clear plastic to be ready to cover the tables, on which he had arrayed the kitchen-type stuff. The tools and hardware, on a tarp on the lawn, could handle a little moisture unprotected.

Light wind with a few sprinkles developed early on, and Uncle Al covered the tables with the plastic. It worked, but he didn't sell much.

About 10:30 the weather eased, and Uncle Al folded up the plastic. He sold a few things before it began to blow much harder and then to rain. In these conditions, things like the tortilla press weren't enough to anchor the sheet of plastic, so Uncle Al tied the ends to the table legs, but the wind kept lifting it in the middle, the rain was getting heavier, and stuff was getting wet.

Around noon, as soon as Uncle Al decided to throw in the towel, so to speak, and start putting things away, it began to pour. He ran into the house with the few items that had to be kept dry, then began to pack all the other stuff into rapidly soggying paper bags. (Memo to self: What had happened to all the empty box after boxes?)

He couldn't put the bags into the open back of the truck for transport to the garage; they'd be sitting there getting wetter until the last of them was packed, and it would take too long to carry them back to the garage two at a time as he filled them, so whenever he got a couple of bags filled, Uncle Al ran them into the living room.

By time the last hardware from the tarp was safely stowed, everything—including the bags and Uncle Al—was really soaking wet, and Uncle Al was exhausted. But he couldn't help noticing that during his rush to get stuff into the house he had apparently left the kitchen door open again, this time giving Fuzzy the opportunity to eat a great many cookies (Fuzzy was now hiding upstairs).

Uncle Al took a shower, did a little rearranging of the mess in the living room, and when the rain began to ease he returned the rented tables, after which he went to his piano lesson on what by then had turned into a sunny afternoon.

He came home to a living room that smelled like a wet dog and a dog who smelled like a wet living room. The idea of schlepping all the wet bags full of wet stuff out to the garage was just too much, but Uncle Al was having company Sunday and he needed to clean and start cooking so the next day wouldn't be frantic.

So he took all the bags . . . back down to the basement. Although he had sold a fair amount of stuff on Friday, the sale included some stuff from the garage that had never been in the basement, so the new pile covered about half the floor—clear back to the door to Dave's room.

But now it was wet.

Kipling on Credit

ᶜᶜᶜ

Editor's note: *We can't find Uncle Al's column, so we've asked poet and fabulist Rudyard Kipling* (Gunga Din, Just-So Stories, The Jungle Book) *to stop being dead long enough to jot down one of his charming little tales.*

So-So Stories
"How the Bank Gets Its Money"

Once upon a time, O Best Beloved, when the century was new and all, there was a man who bought very many things, spending more money than he really had. You might wonder at this, O Best Beloved, but it was not difficult: He had a piece of plastic.

It came from a big fat bank, which kept telling him that he hadn't spent enough money yet.

The man was very foolish and bought more things. "I can't afford all this," he said, "but with this piece of plastic I can pay the big fat bank only a little bit every month! Life is really good!"

But as he spent and spent, the little bit he owed the big fat bank every month grew bigger and bigger, until he owed $4,000, his monthly payment was $117 and his morning latté was at risk.

Then one day he got a letter from a different big fat bank (in those days, Best Beloved, there were several big fat banks):

If he transferred his balance to their piece of plastic, he'd pay no interest for a year. "Done!" he said, and with no interest he paid only $83 a month. Life was good, but he realized that it would take four years to pay the new big fat bank what he had owed the old big fat bank. So he finally stopped buying things. Pretty much.

Before he knew it the year was up, and—just as the rate was to go from zero percent to 17.99 percent— the foolish man got a letter from another big fat bank, offering zero percent for another year. "Done!" he said again, transferring his balance (now down to $3,000) to the third big fat bank.

One night, while he was staring at a thing called "TV" so he wouldn't have to do a thing called "reading," he realized that he was still using the first big fat bank's piece of plastic (to earn miles on a bankrupt airline), and the third big fat bank's piece of plastic (it was giving him zero percent for a year), but he had no need for the one from second big fat bank. So he picked up the phone to close that account.

"O, foolish man," the woman at that big fat bank said, "go tell your wife we'll give you 2.99 percent for a year." He puffed up his chest and declared, "I already have zero percent for a year. And I'm not married."

"O, foolish man," she said, "we can give you zero percent on a balance transfer *forever*. And we just like the sound of 'Go tell your wife.' Tell whomever you please."

Now, the man was foolish but he was no dope; he figured no big fat bank charges zero interest forever without making money somehow. He recalled that some big fat banks charge 3 percent just for the balance transfer. So he puffed up his chest and demanded a no balance-transfer fee.

"O, foolish man, go tell Aunt Rhody we can do that, too,"

the woman said. Then she said three magic words, although the foolish man did not at once see their magic. And the words she said were these: "Here's the thing."

Then she spoke a longer incantation: "The rate will be zero for a year; it will then remain zero every month there is at least $25 of activity on your card, at our usual awful rate, now 17.99 percent. If any month has no $25 charge, your transferred balance permanently goes to that awful rate."

The foolish man calculated: Even at 17.99 percent, the interest on a $25 monthly charge would be 37 cents a month, and the new minimum payment on his $3,000 balance would be $62.50, which would pay it off in four years. The only interest he would pay would be the 37 cents a month, totaling $17.76 over four years. "Sign me up!" he said, wondering at the foolishness of the big fat bank.

To make sure he got the monthly $25 habit going, the man immediately charged half a tank of gas. (In those days, Best Beloved, half a tank of gas cost only $25 or $30.)

And there, he discovered when he examined his monthly statements, was the thing: His entire payment (even the $25 he added, to pay for the gas) was being applied to the zero-percent transferred balance; meanwhile the gas charges were piling up as "purchases," unpaid, compounding at 17.99 percent.

The $3,000 would be paid off in 34 payments (instead of 48). But by then the $25 worth of gas a month would magically have become an unpaid $1,115 ($265 of it interest).

If he then stopped charging but kept paying $87.50 a month, it would take more than a year to pay off, and the total he would pay the big fat bank for the $850 worth of gas would be $1,232.

The zero-percent-forever bargain would cost him $382!

When this zero-percent year ended, the foolish man vowed, he'd stop trying to outsmart big fat banks, and settle for a simple good deal.

Here's the lesson, Best Beloved: If a tiger lets you run away, don't go back and demand a massage.

Gus Enters the Picture, Sitting on the Couch

ᴛᴄᴄᴄ

It's time for a dog update. After the sudden early death of his pal Fuzzy, whom he missed terribly, Uncle Al adopted Billie, a very bright but difficult little dog. One of Billie's bad habits (frequently using the dining room carpet for a purpose not envisioned by its manufacturer) caused Uncle Al to install another door, this one enabling him to close off the dining room.

Billie turned out not to have been a great match for him. She needs to run and chase and be on guard—and to learn a lot of discipline; he needs to sit on the couch—and to sit on the couch.

In short, for a little dog, Billie was a huge handful. And Uncle Al—a single geezer with a full-time job—hadn't enough time or energy to deal with her effectively.

Long story still pretty long, heaven smiled on both Uncle Al and Billie, as the folks at Homeward Bound found her a new home early last month—with a woman who knew all about Billie's problems and fell in love with her anyway. Billie's new owner sent Uncle Al a smiling picture of the two of them; Billie wasn't biting her new owner's hand, which was an improvement already.

Uncle Al then took a break from dog owning, wanting to be more judicious in finding a new dog this time. He decided to figure out the right kind of dog for him; after that he'd find that kind of dog somewhere. (Meanwhile he sanded and painted the dining room door. And shampooed the carpet.)

As part of the winnowing process, Uncle Al took several Internet "What kind of dog?" tests: Do you mind shedding? (No; Uncle Al has come to think of dog hair as a fashion accessory.) How much can you exercise the dog? (A walk to the park; if he wants more he can go up and down the stairs at home.) How smart must it be? (Able to unwind his leash from a telephone pole; Uncle Al will do his own long division.)

All of the tests reinforced the idea of a Corgi (a breed very evident in Fuzzy's background), so Uncle Al started looking for Corgi mixes on Petfinder.com (the website that collects the listings of lots of humane societies, shelters, pet-rescue groups and the like).

Although there were others closer to home, with pleasant-looking pictures and full descriptions, something about a dog in east-central Iowa, with no photo and few details, spoke to Uncle Al. He sent an inquiry to that shelter, asking about the mystery pooch, and describing himself as 63 and not much for exercise, adding that he has a full-time job, so his dog had to be able to handle being alone. He didn't actually say, "I want a dog who wants to sit on the couch with me," but that was clearly the spirit of his inquiry.

The reply said, in essence: This could be your dog.

So Uncle Al loaded his truck with books on tape and drove to Iowa, promising himself not to be stupid: The drive would be pleasant, and he could just look.

But heaven smiled on Uncle Al again (he feels pretty far ahead in the heaven-smiling department recently), and the perfect dog walked up to the front of its cage as soon as Uncle Al came in the door.

Gus is Fuzzy in a cream-and-caramel suit, a bit smaller

and if anything even more laid-back: He leaned on Uncle Al's shoulder for most of the six-hour trip back to Minneapolis.

Gus has enjoyed snoozing all day on the couch while Uncle Al is at work, and snoozing all evening on the couch while Uncle Al snoozes next to him. Gus hasn't been perfect: Now and then when Uncle Al gets home he is greeted by a puddle. (Actually, by Gus and a puddle, Gus's being the far nicer greeting.) But Uncle Al isn't perfect for Gus, either: When Uncle Al eats dinner, Gus doesn't get half.

Anyway, Uncle Al has started carrying dog treats on their walks. When Gus salutes a tree, he gets a treat. It's working; there are fewer puddles at home. But Gus is no dope: He used to begin his walks by heavily watering one tree and hitting a few others sparingly; now he briefly irrigates lots of trees, and as soon as he finishes each one he turns to Uncle Al for a treat.

Occasionally he lifts a leg at a tree, does nothing at all, then comes over for a treat. When Uncle Al only grimaces, Gus gives him a look that clearly says, "Hey, I gave it a shot."

When Gus's cousin Ted, whose daily habits are impeccable, visited recently, all three were out for a walk, and Ted dropped back to garnish a tree. As soon as he was done, he walked ahead—and Gus came over to Uncle Al for a treat! At first Uncle Al thought he had missed Gus either peeing or pretending to have done so. Nope: Gus now asks for a treat every time Ted pees.

Meanwhile, Uncle Al has been limiting potential puddle sites by closing the kitchen, dining room and bedroom doors. And, after discovering one "accident" in the tiny upstairs study—a room paved with stacks of books and paper (mercifully, none of those was involved)—he blocked Gus's access with a laundry hamper, as the room has no door.

This is the third door Uncle Al has had to hang to close a doorway. This time he didn't have to buy the door: It was in the basement, and he'd already measured it. Twice. But it had no hardware, so after he hauled it up one hot day (and showered), he bought hinges and a lock.

Naturally, the hinges didn't fit. But a few minutes with a hammer and chisel would take care of that, and Uncle Al had recently bought a chisel. Had he been able to find it, how nicely that would have worked out!

It was a small job; a hammer and a flat-bladed screwdriver would do. A screwdriver was at hand, and Uncle Al must own five hammers; even if three of them were in the garage (he didn't want to go out in the heat to see), one of the others should have been easy to find. It wasn't (see Uncle Al's treatise on never putting tools away), so he hit the screwdriver with the pipe wrench he found while looking for a hammer.

Having sweated the heavy door onto the hinges and needing badly to take another shower, Uncle Al instead moved on to the lock. He cut open the user-resistant package, turned to the door, and saw that the hole in the door that once held the lock was the size and shape of a piece of toast. A modern, compact cylindrical lock wouldn't work; he'd need to visit a salvage place. Next week. Meanwhile the door didn't latch; he blocked it with the #$@% laundry hamper.

About to take a shower, Uncle Al had one of the insights that make him such a popular man-about-town and after-dinner speaker: Across the hall, the attic door had an old-style lock! He could put that in the study door and block the attic door with the #$@% hamper. Great! (It is no longer clear to Uncle Al why this was better.)

The attic lock fit the study door easily. When he shut the door, the bolt missed the hole in the strike plate, but Uncle Al, having been around himself for 63 years, expected no better.

It had been a long, hot day, so as a stopgap he removed the strike plate, chiseled (or screwdrivered) a larger hole in the doorjamb, latched the door in that, and took a needed shower.

Several days later he suddenly noticed one of those old locks (on a newish shelf in the basement, so he'd put it there himself). Yay! He wouldn't have to go the salvage place. Oh; it had no knobs. So he would.

He tried the lock in the attic door: going to be tight. (Uncle Al didn't realize that although the lock apparently hadn't come out of that door, it might have come out of the study door. Let's not go there.)

That Saturday, Uncle Al went nuts: He bought knobs and located a chisel, a hammer, and a file. He enlarged the hole in the strike plate so the study door latched, chiseled extra room in the attic door for the new old lock, and installed it. The bolt missed the hole in the strike plate by almost half an inch, so he chiseled a new spot for the strike plate and a hole behind it.

Shot the day, but it was done!

And when he came down to the living room, there, wagging, was Gus! And a puddle.

Hot Pursuit of Cooling

ⲥⲥⲥ

On one of Uncle Al's many recent trips to buy plumbing parts, while the weather was lurching back and forth between surprisingly cold and surprisingly muggy, he noticed that the handy branch of a big chain hardware store had stacks of window air conditioners at fairly reasonable prices.

He realized that this meant that springtime had once more come to the Upper Midwest. "That," he thought, "must mean there's only about a week left until summer."

Not a week later, the most recent of his multiple ex-wives, who was about to go out of town, asked him if he would do her a favor and pick up a window air conditioner for her bedroom. She had given up on trying to cool all of her house with one large window air conditioner in the dining room.

"It would be my very great pleasure to take care of that problem for you, as I can think of nothing else to do with my time," he said, or words not quite exactly to that effect, and he described the units he had seen. "Perfect," she said, and handed him a plastic card with a magnetic stripe. "It's a store credit; they owe me $42. Give them that and pay the difference, and I'll pay you back."

Uncle Al knows what you might be thinking. But despite the ex-ness of the wife in question, Uncle Al knew she would pay him. Nor would anything else in the transaction go wrong. Not very wrong, anyway.

He bought the second-smallest of the air conditioners,

which, like everything from toaster ovens to coffee grinders these days, came with a remote control. It had a sleep timer, too. That's actually a wonderful idea for an air conditioner, he mused; you get to go to sleep cool and not wake up freezing in the middle of the night. He also got a $9 lockset to replace a broken one in her house, and he turned in her $42 store credit and put the rest on his credit card.

When his ex-wife got back, she helped him lug it into her house, but not before saying she thought it would be too big. They set it down in the living room, and Uncle Al took a whole day to accept that if she thought it was too big, although it wasn't too big, it was going to be too big.

So he agreed to take it back and get her the smaller one—partly, he had to admit, because he suddenly liked the idea of putting the air conditioner with a sleep timer in *his* bedroom window.

(It's cool on the main floor of Uncle Al's house, but not up in his bedroom, which apparently had been added to the house. Ductwork for heating and cooling air seems to have been added even later, when there was no room to do it well enough that it would actually work.)

So one night after work they lugged his ex-wife's air conditioner back out to his truck and he went back to the store with her so she could buy a smaller one (if she picked it out, it was less likely to need to be returned), and he put it in his truck; he'd install it in her bedroom that weekend, when she'd again be out of town.

She paid for the new one, which had all the same features, and he promised to give her $33 (for her $42 store credit that went into what was to become his air conditioner—minus the $9 lockset).

Then he got to his house, got out of the truck and finally actually pictured trying to lug the thing up to his bedroom.

So that weekend—that *hot* weekend—Uncle Al went back to the store to exchange his air conditioner for the smaller one. Actually, he didn't go to the same branch. The smaller air conditioner that his ex-wife had bought was the last one of that kind at that store; so he took the "big" air conditioner back to a different branch, lugged it in, got his credit card credited for what he'd charged to it, and got a $33 store credit for the difference. Then he walked to that store's pile of air conditioners . . . and found none that small.

While he pondered what to do next, he drove over to his ex-wife's house and installed her smaller air conditioner. That went fairly easily—he needed only one trip to a hardware store to replace a bolt that was part of the mounting bracket but that stuck up so far that the air conditioner rested on it instead of the bracket.

Uncle Al was very proud of himself for bringing the "bad" bolt along; it turned out to be a metric size, which he hadn't guessed, so he saved himself the trip that would otherwise have followed his discovery that a new shorter (but not metric) bolt didn't fit in the mounting bracket.

Anyway, with that installation done, he drove to the store where both the large and small air conditioners had been purchased, and, using the $33 store credit and putting the rest on his credit card, he bought a different small air conditioner. He didn't like it as well as the one his ex-wife got, but by this time, somehow, after 10 years in his house, he suddenly had to have a window air conditioner that very day.

When he got it home, dragged it in, and got ready to install it, Uncle Al saw that it had a different mounting system, one that—because the bottom of a combination window frame runs across his windowsill—couldn't be made to work.

Although that window frame would make it a minor pain to install the mounting bracket for an air conditioner like his ex-wife's, it could be done.

So he called around and found a branch of the store that had some of the "right" air conditioners in stock, dragged the "wrong" one back to his truck, drove (way the heck) out there, returned the wrong one (getting most of the price credited back to his card and a $33 store credit for the difference), and bought the right one, using the $33 store credit and putting the rest on his credit card.

Uncle Al hopes that the big chain hardware store doesn't have somebody whose job is to detect fraud by looking for suspicious patterns in returns, because, like Abou Ben Adhem, Uncle Al's name would lead all the rest: Bought an air conditioner partly with store credit, returned it for credit at a different store, got store credit, bought an air conditioner partly with store credit at the first store, returned for credit to a third store, got store credit and bought an air conditioner partly with store credit. This guy has to be pulling something.

Actually all that Uncle Al was pulling was a long face, because although he was quite correct that the combination window frame made installing the mounting bracket a pain, he was quite incorrect in thinking it would be a minor pain.

The hot, sweaty, unhappy hour of that task, including sawing a chunk out of the %$#@ metal frame, was interrupted only for a run to a neighborhood hardware store—to get a shorter $%#@ metric bolt for the mounting bracket.

But that night, he smiled as he set the sleep timer on his new window air conditioner to turn it off in two hours, when he would be sound asleep.

He was. The sudden silence of the air conditioner stopping woke him up.

The Gravity of Seasonal Change

With the return of cool weather, the coloring of the leaves and the first belch of dusty warm air from the furnace, Uncle Al found himself pausing to take stock. While putting the stock back, he realized that numerous other less obvious but equally significant events occur at this time each year:

- The discovery of expired coupons or the missing screwdriver or bewildering quantities of unidentifiable fuzz in the pockets of the jacket last worn in April.
- The beginning of the probably fruitless search for the windshield scraper. It was bought new last fall because the one from last year (which quite probably was bought new then because the one from the year before last could not be found) could not be found.

(Uncle Al was going to include the matter of the unfindable scrapers from three and four years ago, but he knew he'd be lucky to get that previous paragraph past three editors as it stands.)

- And with the annual relocation of his keys and cell phone from his pants pockets to the newly available pockets in the jacket and the accompanying decrease in the weight of his pants, comes the annual surprise when his suspenders yank his pants up at least an inch. He never seems to remember this, nor the complementary spring lowering of the pants, until each happens.

Uncle Al has been wearing suspenders for years, so he should be accustomed to such things, but especially in years with multiple starts at cool weather and returns to muggy, he admits he feels off balance as his pants go up and down.

As long as he's already uncomfortable, this might be a good time for Uncle Al to explore a suggestion from editors that he occasionally do his column in question-and-answer form. (There's no reason to do it that way, but there's no reason not to, either.)

In addition to the answers, Uncle Al will happily supply the questions.

Q. Your column is easily the best thing in the newspaper. How long have you been writing it?

A. Thank you. That's nice of you to say. I've been doing this column since 1989.

Q. The praise is well deserved. We will not see your like again. Do you find it difficult to fill 20 or 25 inches of space every week?

A. You're too kind. In fact, sometimes the brilliantly insightful Uncle Al column deals with truths so important and complex that it's difficult to squeeze them into as little room as that. At other times, for example this week, what seemed as if it could easily be stretched into a column ran out of gas after six or seven paragraphs.

Q. Do you mean this whole Q&A thing is just a ruse to fill out your column?

A. Well, I wouldn't put it that way, of course, but yes, before I threw away the thing about my jacket and pants, and just started over, I thought I'd try this and see how it went.

Q. It's certainly not going very well.

A. That's not a question!

Q. Sue me!

A. Nor is that! I must insist you get back to praising me and serving up cream-puff questions.

Q. All right. You are delightfully witty and all, but how can you possibly take a whole week to write this piece of drivel?

A. Ah, you misunderstand. It's true that this piece of drivel appears only once a week, but I write several other pieces of drivel, each at least as edifying, for the Thursday Taste section.

Q. That's good to know, I suppose. Turning to other matters, has anything amusing or dumbfounding—the kind of stuff with which you usually burden readers—happened to you recently?

A. That's a really great question. I'm glad you asked.

Q. Thank you.

A. You're most welcome. Yes, in fact, Uncle Al and his new used dog, Gus, are once more playing host to the older—and recently grouchier—small dog Ted while Ted's boss-lady is out of town.

Unlike the last week they spent together, this time Ted didn't growl at Gus every time Gus came within a few feet of him; he seemed to be saving the menacing manner for when it really mattered—whenever Gus, who inhales his own dinner, so much as looked at the dish that belongs to Ted, who is a more leisurely diner.

But late last week, Ted discovered a new cause for irritation:

When Gus is on the couch, he seems to enjoy propping himself up against its back with his hind legs splayed and his forelegs folded up in front of him, a posture that would look right at home if he was next to a paunchy guy in a tank top, who is holding a bottle of beer.

He can do this for only a minute or two, after which he topples slowly to one side. If Ted is on the couch, too, and if Gus keels over toward him, Ted growls furiously.

This happened often enough that Ted finally eliminated the step of waiting for Gus to topple: As soon as Gus propped himself up, Ted growled at him.

It was as if, without reference to cell phones or keys, the falling of colored leaves in an autumn breeze automatically raised Uncle Al's pants.

One Screw Loose

꒞꒞꒞

Uncle Al recently decided to get a better radio for his truck than the no-frills one it came with. His choice wasn't an aftermarket radio (never mind why); he preferred the carmaker's own premium model, which he could have had in the first place.

So (via the Internet) he bought a used one from a used-auto-parts place in Cleveland. (We'll skip ahead past the struggle to convince the "new" radio's electronic security system that it hadn't been stolen from the wrecked truck in Ohio.)

Some people wouldn't try to install a car radio; others successfully do major stuff to their cars. Uncle Al is in the third group: While reassembling the dash, he dropped a screw.

He looked all over for it, but it was gone. He finished, leaving one screw hole empty, and moved on emotionally. He'd look again, or get a new screw, later. Meanwhile it had turned cold, and he was sure the screw would be easier to find next spring.

A few days later, it dawned on him that his feet felt cold, even when the truck was very hot. After a week of increasing awareness of freezing-foot syndrome, he reached down and found no hot air on his feet; it all blew out of the defroster. With hot face and cold feet, the only place Uncle Al felt normal was around his belt buckle.

He knew he hadn't touched the heating system. But the last time he'd had a car with a warranty, LBJ was president, so he didn't know what to expect; he could imagine a fuss about his having had the dashboard apart. So before he took the truck to his dealer to fix the heater, he set out to find a replacement for the missing black hex-head machine screw.

Hardware stores had zip. Auto-parts stores all had the same set of prepacked screws; the only one even close had a Phillips head, not a hex head. Uncle Al finally gave up and bought a pack of those and put one in: The mechanic might take a break just before he got to that screw so he wouldn't notice having to switch from nutdriver to screwdriver.

Uncle Al made the service appointment, and it didn't hit him until he was pulling into the dealership: What if it was the lost screw that had jammed the heat door? Drat! But it was too late to worry about that.

The service manager came out pretty soon: They had verified there was no heat on the floor, but sorry: It would take seven hours to fix. Uncle Al said he'd make a new appointment. But before he did so he'd take the dash apart again and search for the screw with renewed vigor, heightened resolve and a magnet on a stick.

As he started unfastening the dash that Saturday, he glanced into a cup holder and saw . . . the missing screw.

So he hadn't broken the heater! Relieved, he began to put it back together. That's when he dropped another screw.

He looked all over, including in the cup holder many times, but it was gone. So he was back to using the #%$@ Phillips screw, leaving it obvious that he had been in there. So he was also back to trying to find the right replacement screw. It wasn't as if it was really unusual. Every screw in the dashboard was the same.

A sudden flash: He could buy one from a dealer. (Not the

one fixing the heater; the parts guy might have a hot line to the warranty-denial guy.) So Monday he went up to another dealer's parts window and set a "good" screw on the counter.

"What vehicle?" "S-10." *(Click-click.)* "Year?" "2003." *(Click-click.)* Uncle Al was getting a bad feeling: Why was the guy looking it up? Surely the woods (and parts bins) were full of these screws. "Where from?" "Dashboard." *(Click.)*

The guy swung his screen around, displaying an exploded view of the dash. "Which one?" Uncle Al pointed to a screw, saying, "They're all the same." The screen swung back.

(Click-click.) "Well, it's $4.73, and I have to send for it."

"$4.73? For how many?"

"One."

"You're kidding! Four dollars and 73 cents for one screw?"

"Yeah, and you only want one; I have to buy 10 and I'm stuck with the other nine."

There is something deep within Uncle Al that refuses to spend more than $4.72 for one screw, even if it solves a problem. He didn't even consider ordering the screw; he just left.

He drove away, fuming: His truck was full of those screws, and, unless General Motors is run by people even less organized than he is, every 2003 GM vehicle was surely full of the same screw, and almost as certainly, so were many other years of GM vehicles. Any bonehead would want to use the smallest possible assortment of screws.

He didn't know what was up, but a 1½-year-old truck couldn't be full of screws so unusual that if a mechanic dropped one they'd have to send away for it—for $4.73.

Then he had a brainstorm: a junkyard! (That is, an auto recycling center!) So the day after the big snow he headed out to such an enterprise. There he rapidly verified that a screw identical to his except for a slightly smaller flange—he didn't care—was all over every GM dash since the mid '90s.

As long as he was there, and his feet were already cold and wet (he hadn't been able to find his boots), Uncle Al kept looking for newer cars (hard to tell with half the car missing or caved in), as they might have the identical screw. Each time he guessed wrong, he took a couple of the not-quite-identical screws anyway: He might drop another one someday and he would need spares. Eventually he found a newer car and took several perfect screws.

Walking to the office, inventorying his pocket, he was startled to find he'd harvested 21 screws.

He showed his fistful to the guy at the parts counter, saying, "Bunch of sheet-metal screws." Thinking the parts guy said, "Let's see 'em," he spread them out. "No," the parts guy said, "See ya." (Parts-guy talk for "No charge.") Uncle Al thanked him profusely, went out to his truck, and filled the empty spot.

That Tuesday "his" dealer fixed the broken heater door, in the estimated time, under warranty, with courtesy to Uncle Al and utterly without discussion of screws. Now Uncle Al needs to decide what to do with the fraction of the remaining 20 screws that he'll surely never need. So far he has two ideas:

Donate them to his dealer.

Or go to the other dealer and attempt to return them for $4.73 apiece.

Gus Taps into Piano Time

ˇʕʕʕ

Uncle Al is happy to report that Gus has achieved clarity on the difference between the park two blocks away and the living-room carpet.

It's possible that Gus has discovered someplace in the house where he can find relief and not be detected, but a recent incident suggests otherwise:

(Picture Uncle Al and Gus getting all wavy as this flashback begins. This will be the only one; Uncle Al doesn't look too great even when he isn't all wavy.)

One night a few weeks ago, Uncle Al accidentally left a big bag of dog food open on the kitchen floor, left that door open, and sat down to do his piano practice, during which he tries mightily to ignore whimpering and shoulder tapping from Gus.

Yes, Gus—whose tolerance for the piano stylings of Uncle Al usually lasts less than three minutes—has discovered that, when whimpering fails, he can climb onto the back of the couch near the piano, reach out to where Uncle Al is seated on the piano bench, and tap him on the shoulder. Endlessly. This is somewhere between annoying and intimidating. Uncle Al suspects that if Gus is persuaded to stop shoulder tapping, he might switch to clearing his throat.

Anyway, on the night in question Uncle Al suddenly realized that he was neither hearing nor feeling Gus. He looked around, didn't see Gus, and immediately suspected the worst.

Only one thing could keep Gus from protesting the slow torture of Uncle Al's piano playing: food.

He rushed into the kitchen to see Gus pulling his head out of the dog-food bag. As it turned out, he hadn't eaten enough to make him sick that night, and he seemed fine on his walk the next morning, too.

But when Uncle Al came home from work that night, he found that Gus had left behind a sizable reminder of his raid on the dog food bag. It was right in the middle of the only open space in the living room, exactly where he used to have his "accidents." So Uncle Al is pretty sure Gus hasn't hidden other examples; when they happen Gus seems to be oddly proud of them.

And as Gus has settled in, other less-than-delightful bits of dogly behavior also have been on the decline. For example, Gus has almost stopped chewing on things he finds around the house while Uncle Al is at work. This is partly because Uncle Al has installed doors on rooms with particularly irresistible contents (and he usually remembers to close them), and he's provided Gus with plenty of chew toys.

Uncle Al has even worked to reduce the heaps of living-room clutter that might contain items Gus could find toothsome. That's an indication of just how fond he is of Gus: Lots of what Uncle Al removed from the coffee table had been there for months; some of the stuff on the desk went back to the previous century.

Meanwhile, Uncle Al is beginning to notice something else he needs to work on: As did previous dogs, Gus pulls pretty hard on the leash when out walking. Uncle Al knows it's not difficult to train a dog not to do that, but until now he's never minded it very much. However, some combination of Gus's enthusiasm and Uncle Al's increasingly out-of-warranty wrists recently brought the matter to a head.

Uncle Al decided to postpone the patient outdoor training necessary to stop Gus from pulling, at least until the part of the year when his face won't freeze. But as an interim measure he bought one of those special collars that go around the dog's nose and chin. When the dog pulls on the leash, this gizmo pulls the dog's head down; dogs apparently enjoy that even less than bad piano playing, so they stop pulling.

Gus, however, hated the special collar even more than he hated having his head pulled down, and for the entire walk he burrowed along with his head in the snow, trying to get the thing off. All he got was snow up his nose, but that didn't stop him from doing it for six blocks.

When they got home and Uncle Al removed the collar (much to Gus's relief), he tossed it onto the desk and decided not to try it again until there was less snow cover.

The next night, coming home from work, the second thing Uncle Al saw (after Gus, looking nervous) was the collar, lying on the floor next to the desk. It was in three pieces. Gus had neatly chewed through it. Twice.

Uncle Al hopes the piano isn't near the top of Gus's ten-most-detested list. It's been in his family for many years, and he'd hate to come home to find that Gus had chewed through it.

Going Full Throttle Across the Web

ⅽⅽⅽ

Before he says anything else (including this, but it's too late), Uncle Al has to say that he is a very frequent user of information from the Internet. As Mr. Tidbit in the Taste section, he often uses food-related information from the Internet, and as Uncle Al for this column, he often uses peculiarity-related information from the Internet.

He also uses the Internet at home, to read about several hypothetical hobbies (things that might be hobbies if he ever did anything but read about them). Most require that he begin by clearing some space, which for Uncle Al tends to be a hypothetical activity all by itself. And it's one he doesn't even read about.

Anyway, after several unsettling experiences, Uncle Al now notes the Internet source of any facts he gathers—or he selects the source himself—because he has learned a key truth:

In a library, you first choose a reference work, based on what you want to know and your opinion of the choices; then you open it. On the Internet, a search engine presents a list of sites that refer to what you're looking for. You can click one and find an answer without ever noticing who provided it: a reputable source, somebody with an agenda or some guy you wouldn't trust to rake your yard.

Uncle Al is so fond of the Minneapolis-to-Manhattan mileage calculator story—and others about mishearing things on TV (like the unbelievably short 30-second anniversary sale that turned out to be a 32nd-anniversary sale)—that he's begun to wonder if he actually enjoys being confused.

He has decided that he likes confusion best when he can blame it on someone else not having been clear. (Work in progress: "Why Uncle Al is no longer married.")

Anyway, when he searched the Internet recently for some information about Full Throttle, Coca-Cola's new "energy drink," he discovered that even carefully selecting the source of Internet information doesn't necessarily ensure that one will fully understand the information and its context.

From the many Web sites that his search for "Coca-Cola" and "Full Throttle" turned up, he took care to pick that of the Coca-Cola Company itself. (Lots of others were just folks talking about it, or about car racing.)

Thus assured that he was getting the straight poop, Uncle Al found the Full Throttle news he needed. But there was a "new products" link, and he could be interested in other new Coke products, so he clicked it. He scanned the entries; most were familiar (Diet Coke with Splenda, Coke with Lime). But the last one was a surprise:

Coca-Cola, the total beverage company, has launched a highly innovative ready-to-drink canned coffee under the brand name ZU. ZU is expected to shake up the canned coffee segment, and is the first ready-to-drink coffee product blended with ginseng.

Whoa! Coke sells canned coffee? With ginseng? How had that slipped past Uncle Al? He clicked to see the full announcement. It began:

"ZU," the only ready-to-drink canned coffee with ginseng, in November is launching its latest and greatest activity yet, the "ZU Man Search," in key locations around the Northeast . . .

Oh, so maybe it rolled out in stages, starting in the East five months ago. Still, if ZU is all over New York, it's surprising we haven't heard of it. Or maybe it means a year-earlier November. He read on:

The beautiful hostess Nan-Prangwalai . . .

WHO??!

will lead the ZU-ZA Caravan and bring the exciting "ZU Man Search" to the real men in . . .

WHAT?!?

several provinces, starting with Ubon Rachathani . . .

OH! Somehow Uncle Al had stumbled onto a Coke product being introduced in *Thailand*.

It turns out that he had turned up not the Coca-Cola USA site, but the Coca-Cola Company site, where subtle distinctions such as "Is this for sale here or on the other side of the Earth?" aren't important.

(Looking back, the headline did say "ALL OF ISAN" was welcoming ZU, but Uncle Al had read right past that.)

Uncle Al read further, in case there was anything of interest in the rest of the announcement.

There was lots about the ZU-ZA caravan (watch ITV "for real ZU-ZA excitement")—all of it already over (it had happened last November). But for Uncle Al the prize—the kind of Internet gold in pursuit of which he wastes many a happy hour—was the name of the TV show that was to cover the "ZU Man Search": *Poob-Pab-Rub-Choke.*

That words in some language can amuse people who don't speak it isn't high comedy, but *Poob-Pab-Rub-Choke,* as a show for fans of a new coffee-ginseng drink, struck Uncle Al as pretty good. It sounded like noises you'd make if you tried the new coffee-ginseng drink and didn't care for it.

But Uncle Al likes to think that this column promotes an

elevated level of discourse, so he attempted to find out what Poob-Pab-Rub-Choke means.

Searching for that phrase on Google turned up just one match: the Coca-Cola Company site where he found it in the first place. Google's typo detector suggested "Did you mean: *Pub*-Pab-Rub-Choke"? No, but if Google thought that would help, Uncle Al gave it a try.

That way, no matches.

So he contacted his favorite Thai, Supenn Harrison, of the Sawatdee restaurants. She said "poob-pab" means "right away" and "rub-choke" is "get money" or "get reward." Poob-Pab-Rub-Choke is Thai for a Coke "Instant Winner" game.

That's ZU-ZA excitement!

Now all Uncle Al needs to know is the distance between Minneapolis and Ubon Rachathani. And he can find that on the Internet, poob-pab!

To Continue, Press 1

ᗢᗢᗢ

Editor's note: *Al Sicherman is unusually ineffective this week, so we're taking this opportunity to try out a new automated Al Sicherman column. We hope you find it at least as useful as Al's regular column, as we plan to contain costs by switching to this automated service and replacing Al with a mechanically operated wax dummy.*

Welcome to the Al Sicherman column. Please pay careful attention to the following menu of choices, as somebody keeps changing it.

To report your dog lost or stolen, or for a copy of the recipe for tangerine-olive fizz, press 1.

For balance and payment information or for complete rules for the "What Is that Thing in the Pocket of Your Winter Coat" contest, press 2.

To report a delivery problem for today, Monday, press 3.

To request a copy of our catalog of inappropriate T-shirts, press 4.

If you require towing or other roadside service, press 5.

If you're in the middle of the road, and you need to be pushed to the side, press 6.

If you're in the middle of the road, but by that you mean you're neither particularly liberal nor particularly conservative, press 7.

If you can't stand the heat, get out of the kitchen.

To be put on hold for a very, very long time, press 8.

If you know your party's extension, you may press 9, but by this time your party probably has gone home already, unless it's an all-night party.

To speak to a customer service representative, or if you do not have a phone, press 0.

Please wait while we connect you with an operator.

For quality-assurance purposes, and because some of our operators are convicted felons working from their cells and we'd love to catch them stepping out of line one more time, this column may be monitored.

Thank you for reading the Al Sicherman column. All of our operators are busy annoying other readers. Please be patient and your request will be handled in the order it was received. In.

We have been experiencing a very large volume of business due to increased readership of our Al Sicherman column and the resulting large number of complaints about our Al Sicherman column. We're sorry for the delay. Your concerns are important to us. But not so important that we want to hire more operators. In fact, we're laying some off. Thank you.

We apologize for any delay. Including this one. Please don't quit now. You'll be really sorry if you do. We have ways. Please have your Social Security number handy.

There's no reason to take that attitude. We're working as fast as we can. We only have two hands. Each. If you'll just stay on the li—

. . . (ring) . . . (ring) . . . (ring) . . .

—lcome to the automated response center at the popular Al Sicherman column.

Please enter your five-digit ZIP Code, followed by the pound sign because we can't count to five since the accident, and we have no other way of knowing when you're done.

Now please enter the last four digits of your Social Security number, followed by the number of yards in a mile.

Divide by the number of times the letter A appears in the words "Tabasco sauce."

OK, how many deadly sins are there (not counting *Ricki Lake*)?

How many roads must a man walk down before they call him a man?

Please name the Chicago Seven, the Minnesota Eight and the Indianapolis 500.

One moment, please, while we access your accessories.

. . .

—periencing a high volume of readers. We're sure that won't last, so please try again later.

Thank you for continuing to read the Al Sicherman column. We hope you enjoyed it. Be sure to read it again soon.

Two Waggish Tales

⌇⌇⌇

I. The "Carpenter's" Tale

Uncle Al's 31-year-old convertible, which wasn't perfect but was good enough to inspire an occasional "Wanna sell that car?" was stolen not long ago. Uncle Al managed to find a 31-year-old replacement, which is much shinier (it was repainted). It is producing many more of those puzzling offers.

Uncle Al doesn't know why folks who might want to buy an old car don't go looking for one instead of expressing an interest in cars they find themselves next to at stoplights, but there it is.

Anyway, one recent Saturday evening, his new old convertible's top down in the warm night air, Uncle Al had just pulled into the drive-through at a Burger King to get a Hershey Pie when a fellow walked up. . . . At this point, too many people who have seen the Wendy's unicorn ad, and some who haven't, stop Uncle Al to say "Wait! Burger King has Hershey Pies?"

Yes.

Moving on, this guy walked up to Uncle Al (seated in his car) and said, "I'm not a robber or a crook or anything bad. I'm a carpenter. The starter went out on my truck, and I need $4 to . . ."

Uncle Al interrupted, having heard many versions of this story. "Here's a buck," he said, giving the guy the dollar he'd had in his hand to buy the Hershey Pie. (He hung onto the seven cents he had just fished out of his pocket into his other hand for the sales tax.)

"Thank you," the guy said, then, stepping back, added, "Nice car! How much do you want for it?"

Uncle Al's son Dave, on hearing about this, asked, "So did you give him the other $3 because he obviously really was a carpenter, not a panhandler?" No; Uncle Al is of the opinion that carpenters whose starters go out seldom hit up strangers at the Burger King drive-through. But he didn't ask for his dollar back, either.

II. The Shaggy Dog's Tale

Has Uncle Al said that the new old car, though lovely, lacks some of the fine accessories of the previous one? Notably it is without the AM-FM-eight-track stereo, which was the clunky extra-cost sound system in your better 1975 autos. (Note for persons younger than 40: The eight-track is kind of like an iPod, in the same way a stick is kind of like an Xbox.)

Uncle Al has found an intact 1975 Delco AM-FM-eight-track stereo, and he plans to install it when he has a weekend long enough to allow for multiple runs to Ax-Man, Radio Shack and the hardware store.

Meanwhile, he realized one day that many of his eight-track cartridges, a pile built up in the 10 years he had owned the previous car, were stolen with it.

In his tiny mind Uncle Al is convinced that part of the fun of driving an old car is singing along to old music. This has meant that he often sang along with "Be True to Your School" on a Beach Boys eight-track.

Most of his favorite cartridges were chance acquisitions in

bags of miscellaneous flea market eight-tracks. So rather than look for specific cartridges to replace his losses, he bought a box of 140 assorted eight-tracks on eBay, hoping it would contain a few things as memorable as "Be True to Your School."

It arrived a week ago, beautifully packed—bubble-wrap lined and the top cushioned with two big pieces of foam rubber.

Uncle Al set the foam aside (it might come in handy), cleared a table of papers, magazines, car parts, tableware and tools and began to sort the cartridges.

He made two big piles, one for each of the two bad designs embodied by the cartridges' internal parts. (One kind was barely adequate and sometimes came apart. The other wasn't even that good; it just disintegrated. This is one reason that few people today wear earbuds wirelessly linked to eight-track players.)

Then he made smaller piles of cartridges with parts that had already come apart or disintegrated. Finally he picked out still-intact cartridges with unappealing music, to serve as parts donors.

The evening flew by, and at its end Uncle Al put the cartridges back in the box, walked his swell dog, Gus, and went to bed.

Coming home from work the next day, he opened the door to find that Gus had chewed up the two large pieces of foam and was standing in bits of it strewn all over the entryway. It looked as if there had been a snowstorm.

"Gus!" Uncle Al snapped, picking up several handfuls of foam, "Bad dog!" And he added, calming down, "Did you think I wouldn't notice?"

Gus, who is on rare occasion able to cause Uncle Al to speak on his behalf, replied, "Would it help if I said the starter on my truck had gone out?"

Long After Joe's Death,
Grief and a Message Endure

᾽ᶜᶜᶜ

On November 8, 1989, my column appeared not in the *Star Tribune*'s Variety section but on the newspaper's front page. "Dear, dear friends," it began. "This isn't going to be easy."

In that column I told readers about the death of my 18-year-old son, Joe, who fell from his dorm window after taking LSD. I think its message is as relevant now as it was when it first appeared.

Joe was a funny, normal kid who made a bad choice, and I wrote the column to show that the horrible things we read about in the newspaper could happen to any of us—that real, normal people, who have regular lives, full of laughter and hope, are only a lapse of judgment away from tragedy.

I received thousands of letters and cards when this column was first printed, and many more in the long years since. I cannot begin to say how deeply I have appreciated that kindness and support. One note was different: It said, "You wouldn't have written this if it was alcohol."

Of course I would have. It makes no difference what drug it was. Joe took something that seriously impaired his judgment, and in an instant it cost him—and his friends and his family—more than he ever could have imagined.

Alcohol accounts for far more such tragedies than does LSD, and if I were writing this column now I would not make it so focused on the specific drug that was the agent of Joe's death. It isn't about LSD; it's about how a simple bad choice can have a horrible outcome—an outcome whose terrible permanence most people, by the grace of God, cannot fully comprehend.

In sharing this story again, I hope it will give other parents and kids an opportunity to talk to each other about drugs and alcohol—not across the generation that separates them, but through the bonds that unite them, and with a heightened awareness of the fragility of our lives.

Hug your kids.

A Father's Plea: Be Scared for Your Kids
1989

Dear, dear friends: This isn't going to be easy.

Nor is it going to be funny.

My older son, Joe, of whom I was very, very proud, and whose growing up I've been privileged to chronicle occasionally in the newspaper, died last month in a fall from the window of his seventh-floor dorm room in Madison, Wisconsin. He had taken LSD. He was 18 years old.

To say he had his whole life ahead of him is unforgivably trite—and unbearably sad.

I saw him a week before he died. It was my birthday, and he spent the weekend with his stepmother and me. He was upbeat, funny, and full of his new activities, including fencing. He did a whole bunch of very impressive lunges and parries for us.

The next time I was with him, he was in a coffin.

He must not have known how treacherous LSD can be. I never warned him, because, like most adults, I had no idea it was popular again. I thought it had stopped killing kids 20 years ago. Besides, Joe was bright and responsible; he wouldn't "do" drugs. It didn't occur to me that he might dabble in them.

His mother had warned him about LSD, though; she knew it was back because Joe had told her about a friend who had taken it. Obviously he didn't listen to her advice. At 18, kids think they're invulnerable. They're wrong.

Joey was a very sweet, very funny kid. And even before he had anything particularly funny to say, he had great timing. When he was about six, I asked him what he wanted to be when he grew up. He paused, just long enough, and said, "A stand-up physicist."

I went to the mortuary in Milwaukee several hours before the funeral to have a chance to be with him. I spent most of the time crying and saying dumb things like "I would have caught you" and "I would have traded with you." I wish I could say that I sang him a lullaby, but I didn't think of it until several days later. I went ahead and did it then, but it was too late. It would have been too late in any case.

Joe was not a reckless kid. Last summer he turned down my wife's suggestion that the family go on a rafting trip through the Grand Canyon; although he loved amusement-park rides, he thought that sounded too risky. So we went sailing and miniature golfing instead. But he took LSD. Apparently he figured that wasn't as dangerous.

When he was about seven or eight, Joey attended a camp for asthma sufferers. When asked, "What do you do at asthma camp?" he responded, cheerfully, "Wheeze!"

The coffin is always closed in traditional Jewish funerals,

and as I sat with him that morning before the funeral, I minded that. I felt so far from him. I finally decided that I had the right to open it briefly, even if it was against some rule. In fact, I rationalized, Joe probably would like my breaking the rule. So I raised the lid.

He was in a body bag.

I'm not surprised that kids don't listen to their parents about drugs. Adults' standards of risk are different from theirs, and they know it; and they discount what we tell them. But we must tell them anyway.

Joe's aunt, a teacher, says that when you warn kids about something dangerous—something that kills people—they always say "Name one." OK, I will. Joe Sicherman. You may name him, too. Please.

Joe's first job was in Manchester, New Hampshire, where his mother had moved with him and his younger brother nine years ago. He was a carryout boy in a supermarket. One day he came to the rescue of a clerk faced with a customer who spoke only French and who wanted to use Canadian money. Armed with his two years of high-school French, Joe stepped forward and explained, "Madame, non!" She seemed not to understand. That, he said, was when he rose to the very pinnacle of linguistic and supermarket expertise: "Madame," he said, with a Gallic shrug of his shoulders, "augghhhhh!" The woman nodded and left.

Because the coffin is always closed, nobody expected anyone to look inside. There were blood spatters on the body bag.

It's entirely possible that warning your kids won't scare them away from LSD. But maybe it will. I wish I could tell you how to warn them so it would work, but I can't.

This is the generation gap reduced to its most basic: It is parents' worst fear that something terrible will happen to their kids; it is kids' constant struggle to be free of the protection of their parents.

Joe's next job was in Shorewood, Wisconsin, a Milwaukee suburb, where his family moved just before his junior year in high school. It was a summer job as a soda jerk. He confided to me that he worked alongside "a soda idiot" and that his boss was "a soda &#%@." Actually, I think he enjoyed it. He told me one day that he was "acquiring meaningful insights into the Sundae Industry." Like: If you say "yes" to "Do you want a lid on that?" you're going to get less whipped topping.

Traditional Jewish funerals leave no room for the stage of grief that psychologists call "denial." When you leave the cemetery, you can have no doubt that the person is dead. In fact, you might say that these funerals are brutal. I could avoid telling you about it, and spare us both some pain, but I think I owe it to Joe—and to every parent—and to every kid—to let this be as forceful as possible.

When the graveside prayers were over, workmen lowered Joe's coffin into the ground and then eased a concrete cover down into the hole until it covered the metal burial vault. The cover had Joe's name on it. They pulled the green fake-grass cloth off the pile of dirt next to the grave, and the rabbi and the cantor each threw a shovelful of earth onto the vault lid.

Then they handed the shovel to Joe's 15-year-old brother, David.

It occurs to me now that what I might have done is ask Joe what kinds of drugs were around. Maybe my genuine alarm at the reemergence of LSD would have registered with him. I'm certainly going to be less self-assured about how I deal with this subject with David. He's a wonderful kid, too, and while I don't want to smother him, I don't want to assume anything, either.

I didn't take Joe for granted; I think I encouraged him and delighted in him and celebrated with him. But I certainly took his life for granted. Parents must not do that. We must be scared for them. They don't know when to be scared for themselves.

Although his humor had become somewhat acerbic recently, Joe remained a sweet, thoughtful kid. When, as I often did, I wound up apologizing to him because a weekend or a vacation hadn't worked out the way I'd hoped, he always patted my hand—literally or figuratively—and let me know he loved me anyway.

He took good care of others, too. He spent most of his grandfather's 90th birthday party making sure that his stepmother had somebody to talk to besides my ex-wife's family.

And on that last birthday visit with me in early October, he talked a little about his concerns and hopes for his brother. One of those concerns was drugs.

Then they handed the shovel to me.

Later I overheard my wife say that the expression on my face when I turned away, having shoveled dirt onto my son's coffin, was the most awful thing she'd ever seen.

Whenever I thought about Joe recently, it was about college and independence and adulthood, and his latest involvements: his attempt to produce an English paper that was more interesting than what the instructor had asked for, the raucous rock band he and his friends put together over the summer, his plans to rent a cabin with a bunch of kids at winter break.

Now, suddenly, I'm no longer looking at the moment, but instead at the whole life. And in some automatic averaging-out, in my mind I'm sometimes calling him "Joey," his little-boy name.

He told his mother a year ago that he wanted his senior year in high school to be the best year he'd ever had, and on the drive to Madison to start college this fall, he told her that, despite lots of typical teenage domestic tension, it had been. He said he'd accomplished everything he'd set out to do—except to have a mad, passionate affair with a woman he didn't even know.

She refrained from asking the obvious question.

Then they handed the shovel to his mother.

Even though it is only three weeks since his death, I find that the reality of Joey is beginning to turn sepia. He will be forever 18. And his life will forever stop in 1989. That saddens me so much. It's not just that he won't have a career, maybe get married, have kids, all those things we hope might happen for a promising young person. He won't go out for pizza anymore either, or come into a warm house on a cold night, or imitate Martin Short imitating Katharine Hepburn, or scuff through piles of leaves.

And I won't ever see him again.

Joe had been very involved in high school journalism. He won a statewide award for feature writing in New Hampshire, and he was news editor of the school paper in Shorewood. He contributed a great deal of that paper's humor edition in May, including a large advertisement that read, in part:

"Attention! All available slightly twisted females: Marry Me! I am a nice guy, a National Merit semifinalist, devastatingly handsome, relatively inexpensive, housebroken, handy with tools, easily entertained, a gentleman in the truest sense of the word, and I think I am extremely funny. In fact, I think I am the funniest guy on earth! . . . Please call immediately. Operators are standing by. (I am in great demand.) . . . Kids—Please get permission from your parents before calling."

Then they handed the shovel to his stepmother.

In his sermon at David's bar mitzvah last year, the rabbi used a phrase I'd never heard before. It caused me to weep at the time; I wasn't sure why. It's come back to me again and again recently. It isn't consoling, nor even helpful. But it is pretty, and in an odd way it puts events into a much larger perspective:

"All things pass into mystery."

At one point during that last visit, we went to a craft fair where Joe noticed someone selling hammered dulcimers. He had never played one, but he'd played the guitar for quite a few years, which must have helped. He picked up the hammers and began to fool around, and soon he drew a small crowd with something that sounded like sitar music. He asked about the price; they were expensive. I keep finding myself thinking that it would be neat to get him one. I should have done it then.

Then they handed the shovel to his only living grandmother; it took her two tries to get enough dirt on the shovel. Neither of his grandfathers could bring himself to do it. But many of Joe's friends, weeping, took a turn.

I hope someday to be able to write about Joe again; I probably won't be writing a humor column for a while. In the meantime, I want folks to know how I think he would have turned out. He would have been a *mensch*—a decent, sincere man, the kind you're proud to know. He already was. Damn drugs.

A year or so ago, the four of us played charades, a vacation tradition. Joe drew The Sun Also Rises, *which he did in one clue. He stretched an imaginary horizon line between his hands then slowly brought his head above it at one end and traversed an arc, grinning from ear to ear. It took us about five seconds to get it. Body bag or no, that's how I want to remember him.*

The last thing I wrote about him appeared in the newspaper the morning he died. He told me that he and a friend decided one Saturday afternoon to hitchhike to a rock concert near Milwaukee. He realized, he said, that now that he was away from home, he didn't have to ask anybody if he could go or tell anybody that he was going. He just decided to do it, and he did it. I wrote about what a heady experience that was, to be independent at last.

There's a fair measure of irony in that column. We're told that the rock concert is where he got the LSD, and where he took his first trip.

That trip, I understand, went OK. This one killed him.

Although Joe apparently was with friends most of the evening, the police said he was alone when he went out the window. We'll probably never know exactly what happened in those last minutes, but judging by our own reading of him and by what lots of others have told us, we're sure he wasn't despondent. Many of his friends, including one who spoke at his funeral, said that he was very happy and enjoying his life in Madison.

The likeliest explanation we've heard is that he had a hallucination—perhaps he thought he could fly. Or maybe he just leaned out too far to see the pretty stars. In any case, a little after 1 o'clock Sunday morning, October 15, somebody studying across the courtyard saw a curtain open and then a body fall. Joe didn't cry out.

I have since, many times.

Hug your kids.